DEAREST WAIKI

Love Letters to an Andean Mystic

MARILYN MARKHAM

INTI WASI PUBLICATIONS

DEAREST WAIKI
Letters to an Andean Mystic

Inti Wasi Publications
408 S. Alarcon Street
Prescott, AZ 86303

Editor: Bob Dyer
Book Design: Christina Watkins and Amanda Summers
Book Production: Becky Fulker
Printed by Classic Prescott Printing, Prescott, Arizona, on archival paper with soy-based inks.

Front cover photographs:
Top—Western Ausangate, Craig Lovell
Q'ero weaving detail courtesy of Al Petrich
Bottom—Thumb Butte: Sharlot Hall Museum Photo, Prescott, Arizona
Night Sky: Frank Zullo

Back cover photograph: Carla Woody

Library of Congress Catalog Card Number: 2003115058
ISBN 0-974628-61-1

A portion of the proceeds from the sale of this book will benefit the Q'ero and Mollamarka Indians of Peru.

I dedicate this book in the name of Love
and for the movement of Salk'a on the planet.

For Mark

Remember that love, in its highest meaning,
is the most powerful gift in the world—
keep it flowing.

Maziebelle Glover Markham

Declare Love,
Act on Love
and be a
Witness to Love.

Marianne Williamson

Contents

Preface

The impetus for this anthology of letters, stories, prose and meditations was a bit of verse I wrote for Don Américo Yábar, my mentor, teacher and friend (pg. 58, *Letter to Waiki*). Don Américo is an internationally recognized poet, mystic and shaman, from the Eastern slope of the Peruvian Andes. I first met him in May of 1997 in the southern wilderness of Utah, where I was drawn to a retreat he was teaching on mysticism and shamanism. I have been fascinated with shamans, their visions and dreams, ever since I was a child. Before the retreat, I gave psychic readings and explored other forms of energy work. Note the emphasis on "work"; I had yet to learn how to allow Divine Love to flow through me, to be a vessel, or a conduit.

Don Américo was to open in me the wonder of connecting to the Power of the Cosmos. He taught me the necessity of "peeling the onion of the Ego," for the service of humanity. It was the simplicity of the method that attracted me; the beauty of the Love with which he walked that spoke to my being. From beginning to end, he held the group with his Love, while teaching us simple ceremonies that focused on cleaning the mind, body and spirit.

I have made four journeys thus far to Perú to work with the *Q'ero Indians*[1] and Don Américo. It was after my second trip, once home and integrating the changes wrought by my travels, that I wrote a letter to him, telling him of my love for his work, my appreciation of all that he is and does, and above all, that I recognized it was my work also. With that recognition, I made a commitment to the awakening of Love on the planet, serving in a way I had yet to discover. His English is not as good as his Spanish, so I had the letter translated so he could fully appreciate my gratitude. Upon his return to the States in the early summer of 1998, I had the pleasure of reading him the poetic translation. On our drive to Prescott, he was speaking about the beauty

---

1   Q'ero Indians: the last surviving Inca. See glossary for more details.

of the prose when he became very excited. He exclaimed "That's it! You can write a book! A book of letters! Letters about everything—the mountains, the children, your people, your life, everything!"

I knew in that instant Don Américo had the right idea. Exuberantly, we began to plan. We laughed and threw around ideas and stories, the things of which I would write. He would, of course, provide the energy. Don Américo's contribution is an indescribable, yet physical and integral part of this book. I felt his energy when the muse would dry up, when I felt doubt anyone would want to read it, let alone publish it. He has been there for me as an assistant to Spirit as it flowed through me to become the written word, knowing the importance of the work and keeping me going in my moments of darkness and doubt. The beautiful energy of the *waikis*[2] was with me when I wrote the beautiful pieces, the sad ones, the ecstatic stories. They are with me all the time.

The course of this book has been like other aspects of my Path; an ongoing litany of questions. Hiking Thumb Butte, our local landmark, I meditated on what I really hoped people would get out of it. What was my dream, my vision? As my feet propelled me down the steep trail, I asked myself, "Why am I writing this book?" "What is its purpose? Who am I wanting to touch?"

The purpose for writing the book is simple: it needed to be written. As to who I want to touch, I want to touch as many people as possible! I've felt for as long as I've been writing this opus that there was something for everyone in these passages, some inspiration or reassurance. I felt others could relate to a particular experience of mine and acknowledge, "I've felt that way before," or "I had some-thing like that happen to me once." In addition, I hoped that my own learning on the Path of Life would teach individuals how to be more genuine, loving and compassionate. There are extraordinary experi-ences and spiritual realities shared here that others may never have. But like me, there are many people who have had inexplicable experiences and either had no one to discuss them with or felt they would be judged or ridiculed if they spoke about the experience to a friend or loved one.

It is my firm belief that fear is the explanation of why so many of us don't discuss nonordinary happenings. Fear of ridicule, judgment, ostracism or worse. Crazy. Touched. So many negative connotations

---

2   waikis: (why'kee) in this case, the Q'ero Indians with which I've worked, and the Mollamarka Indians, both from the highlands of Perú. It is an affectionate term, meaning brother or sister.

for something as simple as . . . conversing with angels. Many organized religions tell us there are angels in the heavens flying down among us. Then why can't we talk with them? Why must we be labeled crazy if we believe the dogma of our chosen religion, thus listening and conversing with these angelic hosts?

The *Encyclopædia Britannica*[3] says of angels: ". . . angel is the equivalent to the Hebrew of the word mal'akh, meaning 'messenger.' Thus, angels have their significance primarily in what they do rather than in what they are." This is exactly what my guardian angel Fernyl is, a messenger. He came to tell me there are many angels, spirits and guides and to tell everyone that "they" are here to help. When many religions teach us there are angelic or otherworldly beings for our assistance, why are we taught to think only special, holy people can converse with them? It is concepts such as this that I hope the reader will find inspirational and something with which they can connect.

As the book neared completion, friends and professionals began peppering me with questions: "Who's your target audience?" "What do you want to say, what do you want people to walk away with?" These are all appropriate and valuable questions, ones that many writers have had to answer. But energetically, I couldn't. I wrote this book on trust and faith, and just couldn't connect with these right-sided, rational questions. I trusted in Spirit when I wondered how I'd pay the mortgage or if anyone would want to buy the book. I trusted Don Américo's keen eye and love of the few pieces I had translated for him. I trusted because Spirit said, "Write the book, just write the book," whenever doubt and concern would crop up. I kept the faith that there were many people who could connect with the stories and letters, and be touched by the Love presented here. And I still have faith that there are concepts and realizations that others will walk away with that I can't possibly imagine. I have to trust and keep faith, because to do less would not be "walking my talk."

Then came the question about how to break up the stories into sections; to make it more manageable for the reader. Would seasons of the year work? Seven is a prophetic and important number for me, can I divide it that way? What are some of the common themes that run throughout? Most of the recommendations I received were geared toward marketing and a message. But to be honest, I have no specific message, other than if you want to live your life with Love for all

---

3   *The New Encyclopædia Britannica*, 15th Ed., p. 871.

sentient beings, you must do it with intent. Love and intent. These two themes certainly run throughout the book. In the end, unable to divide the stories utilizing what felt like a gimmick, I divided it into four chapters and kept the chronological format.

Don Américo and Spirit have guided me along the way, to bring this story of one person's spiritual journey to you. Perhaps the stories may provide a springboard for your own spiritual growth. At the very least, may you connect with it, and find it useful, amusing and spiritually titillating.

Acknowledgments

To all the waikis on the planet, especially Don Américo Yábar, Velquis Yábar and their children, Arilu and Gáyle Yábar. To Milton Johnson, for introducing me to Don Américo's work. To Tom and Bobbi Best, who held the train for me. To Doña Maria, Abelino, Miguelito, Pasqualito, Hipólito, Gabina, Maritza, Gumercinda, Enrique, Fernando, Christian, Doña Feliciana, Don Martín and all the others who make this planet such a vital, vibrant place to live. Thursday evenings with Carla Woody, your ability to put into words what the rest of us are going through never ceases to amaze me. To my family, it took you a while to decide if you liked the new me, but you never stopped loving me. To my son, Morgan Gilliland, you never doubted I could converse with angels. To my husband Al Petrich, you believed in me, trusted in me and encouraged me, all the way to The End. To everyone else, you know there's not enough room in the world to thank you all.

The greatest thanks to my mother, Jonne Markham, without whom I wouldn't know to say "WHOM," among other things. She continues to share with me the beauty of the written word along with her exquisite generosity and love. Goodbye, Dad, and thank you for giving me the joy of reading.

To my readers, many thanks. Carla Woody, Ann-Lawrie Aisa and Joanne Robertson, your feedback was invaluable. Carla Riedel, your added assistance made the writing stronger.

Last, but certainly not least, thank you to Bob Dyer, for being the gentlest editor I could hope for. Thank you for being the technician you are, knowing when to toss out the rules, and for sharing all those great quotes; I won't forget. You are another example of the myriad ways God speaks through us all.

ONE

Now or Never

Mort's Story

My Dearest Waiki,

This first story of Mort, the spiritual traveler who introduced me to other realities, is the necessary introduction to our book. With deep kindness and Love, he prepared me for our eventual meeting. Mort's gift to me was the realization that there are many ways to express Love in this very large universe of ours; some are more easily explained than others. It is the same gift you offer so eloquently and lovingly to thousands of people on our planet. Mort unlocked my heart little by little, always just enough so I wasn't scared by the enormous possibility of our soul's Love. I was ready for a big heart opening when I met you, so you reached right in with both hands and removed its boundaries—much to my amazement and delight. It is now my job to continue where you left off. Both for myself and others.

May 25, 1997

First day of Don Américo Yábar's retreat in the San Rafael Swell of Utah: What an incredible experience! So much energy has moved back and forth, has been felt, seen and heard. I've seen light filaments[1] on the rocks and mountains. My breath has ceased in meditation, while my mind was observing and taking note of no resulting discomfort or concern. I breathed deeply when it seemed time. Wind and rain . . . little sun . . . joyous group. We came together last evening for the first time, so tonight was our second night together, already there is much love and camaraderie.

I am prompted, however, to write on a wholly different topic. My dear friend and spirit guide, Mort, has left this physical world and has gone in a circular swirl of stars. He said it was his time. He insisted I write the story.

It was fall 1973. A senior at boarding school, I was rooming with

---

1   filaments: light, energy, similar to, but not, an aura.

my friend, Leia. Our room was a senior girls' dorm room at the north end of Mr. Campbell's house. It was a separate room, away from the other dorms, with its own entrance.

Over the years, there had been stories about the room, of odd goings-on, noises, even a mirror that cracked in a perfect circle. These were said to be caused by the ghost of Mort, a ranchhand, who died years before. The stories seemed adolescent and harmless, and I paid no attention to them.

On three consecutive nights in the middle of October, I was awakened at 2 a.m. I remember wondering why I was suddenly awake, at exactly the same time each night. The third night, though, was different. When I awoke this night, I could hear what sounded like a violent windstorm—but it was not outdoors. This whirlwind seemed to be right there in my bedroom. My bed was next to the window, so, with every bit of courage I could summon, and in terrified slow motion, I lifted the curtain to look outside. The calm was unbelievably eerie.

Stuttering, I called to my roommate: "Le-, Le-, Leia!" She was known to sleep through almost anything. But she sat bolt upright, saying "What's happening here?"

"I don't know, but I think we should leave." With that, we gathered our blankets around us and fled.

"What was that?" she asked.

"I have no idea."

"Have you ever felt such a wind?"

"What could it have been?"

We got nowhere, other than tripping around in the middle of the night, wrapped in blankets, asking each other questions. After 30 minutes we returned, both feeling it was okay to check our room once again. There was a slight breeze in the trees outside; inside was still and quiet. The atmosphere was clean, calm, peaceful, even inviting. Within a short time we both were fast asleep.

Over the next few days we discussed the experience with each other, but not with adults. God knows what they'd do! So we kept the story to ourselves, and went about our school lives.

Two weeks later, I experienced a very strange feeling one evening as I was falling asleep. There was a great but gentle pressure on my torso, gradually increasing, then covering my entire body. I couldn't speak, and it was very difficult to move my limbs. Oddly, I had no fear, just minor doubts about my sanity, plus an absolute certainty that I would not tell anybody about this experience. The wind was one thing, because Leia could verify that, but this was impossible to explain.

Over the next couple of months, my association and increasing awareness of this being grew stronger. He (I felt strongly it was a male energy) would come to me sporadically at first, then I learned I could bring him to me by asking. This was all done telepathically, a system we worked out naturally along the way. The feeling I experienced with him was what I now know as a particular state of bliss and loving energy. At the time, there was a strong part of me that worried what others would think. Besides that: Was this real? I knew that I liked how I felt with this experience, but I certainly didn't know why.

Over the years, Mort and I developed quite a relationship. Yes, over time, he did tell me he was the spirit of Mort. Not the ghost, mind you, but the spirit, and I could visit with him anytime I wanted. It wasn't really that often, and as my life became more complicated with work, marriage and a child, our visits fell in number. But not in intensity. Every visit was stronger and more vibrant, more physical than the last. I was in my mid-twenties then, and there were only a few people who knew the story. For the most part, I kept it to myself.

In recent years I have found myself connecting with the spiritual side of my life, knowing that this will continue to lead me to love and bliss. I have acquired more helpers in my spiritual life—various angels and other spirit guides—and they have told me their reasons for working with me. I realized Mort and I had never discussed this. So, a year ago, I asked him. We never really conversed, just experienced each other's energy. I was curious about his purpose in my life.

"Yes, as we discussed before, I was Mort. I was not just a spirit that was unhappy or lost. I was waiting for you."

"Me, specifically?"

"Yes."

"Why?"

"So when other guides and angels started coming and telling you it was time to do your work, you wouldn't be scared. We succeeded, eh?"

I swear, he laughed.

So this was the reason. To prepare the way. God and Spirit move in such perfect ways, always such little steps, one after the other.

In the last six months, there has been a shift in Mort's energy. He is more distant. He does not always come when I ask, and rarely does he come on his own. But much is changed now, which brings me back to tonight.

The night was cold and I hadn't been able to get warm at the fire. I had just settled in my sleeping bag and was beginning to gather the warmth of the down around me. Immediately, I noticed that my entire torso was warm. I realized this wasn't the warmth of the sleeping bag, but that of an old, familiar, gentle presence. Excitedly, I welcomed back my old friend, Mort. It is hard to explain the difference between thinking and the connection I have with him. It is much faster and more of a feeling than a thought.

I told Mort that I was concerned about his absence, that I felt him pulling away, and feared his lifetime contract could be coming to a close. I have thought about this in my normal, waking hours. These are not nighttime ramblings.

"It is my time to go," he told me. "You are in good hands as you begin a new aspect of your journey." A wailing erupted from my throat, and I felt as though there were a hole in my heart, with the realization that this loving, warm, physical presence would be with me just this one last time.

"No, no! I'm not ready!"

"Of course you are, you're in good hands; you'll do fine." Back and forth I argued.

"I know it's your time. I know you want to go, but . . . ."

"Just talk to me like always . . . ."

He was calm and reassuring as I wailed and complained. I was faced with the loss of my best friend.

Finally, I paused for breath and as I did, I saw his spirit climb in a spiral of blue, gold, yellow and white lights, ascending toward the stars. The stars! There had been nothing but clouds there just minutes before! I spotted two bright stars next to each other. "That's us, Mort, you and me. Together forever."

"Of course," came the reply. "I'm always here, just differently."

That set off another crying spell, with me apologizing for not expressing more joy for his bliss or my thankfulness for all he had taught me. Then I realized that this, too, was okay. That would come in time, and at this moment I was allowed my grief.

"Besides," he assured me, "when you realized I wasn't around so much, who do you think was helping with your writing?"

He is always here, just differently. Amen.

The following day, shaken by the night's experience, I sought out Tom, Américo's friend and translator. Not sure what to do with my grief, I confided in another for the first time in years. Tom suggested I find the answer in meditation. But he also told me it was necessary to share the fact of my grief with the rest of the group. They could feel it and take it on as their own.

At midmorning we met in a soft, dry creek bed to learn how to clean each other's filaments. You (Américo) talked for awhile and we shared stories. I told the group of my loss, but not the cause. We moved forward with our learning.

Creating *p'uncos*[2] of light, we tap, we clean, we sweep away to *Pachamama*[3] the *hucha*[4] of each other's bodies[5]. I am tired. Many people in our p'unco . . . hot sun . . . I'm thinking too much, working too hard. I have yet to understand about being a clean channel without ego for Love to flow through. I am at Linda's feet. Fleeting thoughts about Jesus and feet move past like wisps of mist. Raising my hands to connect with the essence of the Cosmos, I bring the Power into the right hand, transforming it with Love to the left, as I clean myself in preparation for charging Linda with the vastness of creation. My hands crossing my body in the act of cleansing, and again I raise my hands as if to say "I'm ready."

Stunned, with a whirlwind of thought, feeling, faster than light-speed awareness, I now understand why Mort has left. Here in my hands, all in and around me, I feel that familiar, loving presence. The Love that I experienced for so many years from Mort was now mine to pass on. He left me to my own work of moving the energy, giving the Love of the Universe, to others.

Joyfully, I moved to touch my dear friend's feet.

---

2   p'uncos: pools of light, literally translated as pools of fish.
3   Pachamama: Mother Earth.
4   hucha: heavy energy.
5   . . . each other's bodies: a description of cleaning another person's physical and energetic body.

My First Teacher

September 1995

My personal life was a mess. I kept choosing men who drank too much and were emotionally unavailable. All the signs were there, in full living color. I just kept ignoring them.

I was lying on Juanita's massage table, receiving a birthday gift, sobbing. "Why can't I see what's right in front of my face? I want love so desperately I refuse to listen to what a man is telling me, assuring him all along 'It'll be all right!' I've got to figure out why I keep doing this. I've been through enough therapy to last me a lifetime. I need to find some different answers, a different way of operating."

Juanita just commiserated, not denying what I was saying because she knew it was true. Feeling desperate, I thought of something that had aroused my curiosity in the past, but didn't feel it was for me.

"Do you know about that psychic that lives in Oregon? Deedie and a few other people have gotten readings from him, over the phone." I knew things were grave if I was considering a psychic—but there you have it.

"Well, I don't personally know that man, although I've heard the family talk about him. I do know a woman, Ellen Solart; she lives at Arcosanti." Juanita promised to get Ellen's phone number and call me in a few days.

That same evening we had a birthday party for all of our Virgo friends. There was quite a crowd, including Juanita. Most of them were latter-day hippies or at least yuppies, so when I saw a woman in a red dress with matching shoes and purse, she stood out and grabbed my attention. Surprisingly, I didn't know her. After 33 years in Prescott, I thought I knew almost everyone. There was something else I couldn't quite put my finger on.

"Who's the woman in red?" I asked Juanita.

"Oh! That's Ellen; the lady I was telling you about this afternoon."

Was this a turning point in my life? Without a moment's hesitation, I marched up to Ellen.

"Hi. My name is Marilyn Markham, and I understand you're a psychic."

"Yes." Her response was hesitant.

"Well, I'd like to call you and have a reading. I'd like to be able to work with you." Even as the words tumbled out of my mouth, I wondered: "Work with you? What does that mean?" I left the party with Ellen's card and plans to meet in the future.

Three weeks later, I went to her home near Arcosanti. The 45-minute drive gave me plenty of time to think about why I wanted to see her. She had suggested that I examine my reasons for seeking her out. What did I want to know? I had always had a strong sense of "knowing," and sometimes I would sense that something was about to go wrong even before it happened. Sometimes, as a friend began to describe an object or place, I would anticipate the words with a mental vision that turned out to be uncannily accurate.

I wanted to have greater . . . what was the word I was looking for? Control? No, I knew I had to be careful with my words, more selective in my phraseology in this new dimension of my life. No, not control. Access! That was it! I wanted greater *access* to this new dimension of my life. I also knew I was devastated by my inability to trust, to know the right person to trust, to trust my own judgment. In short, I was miserable enough to change.

Ironically, the reading itself was not life-changing at all. Rather, it was the realization that followed, based on Ellen's view of how my life was progressing at that moment. I wasn't able to trust anyone else *because* I couldn't trust myself. So simple; yet so difficult. So that was how we began working together, teaching me to trust myself and to trust the inner voice we all have.

There was, however, one special aspect to that initial reading. Ellen was bringing it to a close when she suddenly exclaimed: "Oh! There is a very strong energy here that wants to tell you something. She is an elderly woman with kind eyes and white, wavy hair. She is putting a long, blue cloak of velvet around your shoulders and she is saying, 'You're on the right Path, now, Precious, I know you'll do fine.'" As the tears of joy mixed with sorrow coursed down my cheeks, and the name "Precious" sank in, I quietly answered "Thank you, Grandma." Although Grandma used that title for many loved ones in our family, no one else ever called me "Precious." Since her death I never felt she had left me, and I always talked to her when in a quandary. It was reassuring to know that she really was there.

The greatest gift that Ellen Solart gave me in the year that we actively worked together was the gift of reassurance and trust. She taught me how to find my inner voice, how to listen to it, trust it and feel the reassurance that comes from that. All that she taught me— meditation, decision-making, moving energy, intuitive readings of many kinds—these can only be accomplished with trust in yourself and trust in the Universe. The accompanying beauty and reassurance in your life is the intangible reward. I have thanked her before, but it gives me great pleasure to thank her here, for being my first teacher; fine, funny and eminently trustworthy.

Heartaculture

Heartaculture™ is a term coined by my first teacher and mentor, Ellen Solart. It is a way of life, of following your heart and your inner guidance. It is doing only what you truly want to do. Heartaculture™ takes practice.

Clarification is necessary here. Heartaculture™ is not about lying around, expecting the Universe to provide. Nor is it behaving irresponsibly and ignoring obligations. It is learning to listen to your own inner voice and then following its guidance. I picked a day with few obligations to keep track of my practice, and will use that as an illustration.

My radio alarm generally went off at 6:30 every morning. In the past, I would stretch out the time to almost 7:15 before I got out of bed, thus making the morning with my 13-year-old son, Morgan, a bit rushed. Using Heartaculture™, I chose to get up at 7:00, consequently feeling a bit luxurious, but not rushed. Morgan and I then had a relaxed time together getting him ready for school. There was plenty of time for showering, making his lunch and getting him to school on time.

Later, after returning home, I was having an involved telephone conversation with a friend. I was happy to continue our discussion in that way, but she abruptly said "Well, are you going to come over and we can continue this then? I have things to do and we can continue talking while I straighten my house." It was clear that she intended to stop our conversation immediately. Feeling a bit thrown, I realized in the past I would have said, "Okay. I guess I'll come over." But that's not what I wanted to do. So, armed with my new way of operating, I politely declined and went about my morning.

This may seem like a petty example, but for me it was the beginning of not only standing up for myself, but of really paying attention, without question, to that uncomfortable feeling in my chest or stomach.

The day proceeded uneventfully, with small decisions about food, coffee, exercise and the like. In the afternoon, I had to make a trip downtown to the post office and bank.

The following week I related my day to Ellen. About going downtown, I told her, "I didn't really want to go, but I had to. I'd promised someone I'd put something in Priority Mail and I needed to make a payment that was already a day late."

Ellen was amused. "No," she said, smiling. "You didn't have to do those things."

"Yes, I did! Someone was counting on receiving information in the mail from me in exactly three days and my payment was late! I had to!"

"No," she replied. "You see, Marilyn, you're a reliable person and made a friend a promise. You didn't want to let them down. In addition, it matters to you that you have good credit, so you didn't want the payment to be overdue. In short, you wanted to do these things. It's not about just doing completely what we want to do; it's about learning the motivation for doing them. It helps us to see there are a lot of the things we do that are more of 'we want to' than 'we should.'"

Instantly, I had a completely different attitude toward grocery shopping. Armed with new awareness, I noted, "I really like having a full pantry, and enjoy being able to prepare almost anything with little notice. But I don't like the drudgery of the once-a-week, 45 minutes of shopping. It's so boring! But if I go more often for shorter periods of time, then maybe I won't dislike it so much."

Ellen concurred and I was excited about the possibilities. Many old habits have been changed by listening to my heart.

Another way of learning to listen to your inner voice can be as simple as driving. For example, you're taking the same way to work as you do every morning. Some little voice suggests you take a different route. You almost "see" in your mind's eye the alternate route. You decide to listen to that voice and subsequently get to work on time, never knowing what it was about. Or, as usually happens when we ignore that voice, you might get stuck in traffic, or have a driving altercation that leaves you angry and out of sorts. If we're lucky, this is all it amounts to.

My experience has been this sort of thing: My sister and I were driving to Phoenix for a weekend of fun and relaxation as our

Mother's Day treat. She had picked the hotel and I was driving. We had been on the interstate just a few minutes when I thought to ask her exactly where we were going, so I would know what turnoff to take. As I turned to question her, I saw her immersed in paperwork, so I decided to wait until we were further down the hill. As we approached north Phoenix, I interrupted her.

"Janet, where is it we're staying? How do we get there?"

Surprised we had gone so far already, she responded: "Oh dear! We could have taken the Carefree Highway back there; it would've been faster . . . ."

We had passed that exit a few miles back. I should've listened to my intuition at the top of the hill. Sometimes we get off lightly; sometimes we don't. It is really important to listen to the Universe. It will keep at you until you hear what it's trying to tell you, and if you ignore it for too long it can be very unpleasant!

One last point about Heartaculture™. As Ellen had said, it is about discovering our motivation for doing something. The intent is to make our Path easier and more joyful. Here's another example: I had agreed to move my son from his school of five years to a different school, with only six weeks left in his eighth-grade year. Now, if you were to ask if this was something I really wanted to do, I probably would have said "No." But my larger motivation was for his happiness and the opportunity for a positive learning experience. Because he had been so miserable at his previous school for so long, we made the move.

We must learn to take care of those around us by using our hearts, in addition to taking care of ourselves the same way. Sometimes this means turning down social obligations, job offers that don't fit, or any other "should." The "should" may very well be fulfilling someone else's expectations, as opposed to following our own heart and our own Path. It's not always easy, but then nobody ever said it would be! At least, with Heartaculture™, you know for sure you're making the right decisions, both for your heart *and* for your soul.

My Guardian Angel Knocks

My Waiki,

My first encounter with things that go bump in the night brought Mort to me. Maybe it's a theme in my spiritual life, as another useful and loving aspect of Spirit made its presence known in a startling and noisy manner.

Spring 1996

My idea of insomnia is when I take more than ten minutes to fall asleep. I had just gone to bed and was settling in for a good night's sleep. Relaxing, adjusting my pillow, letting the day dissolve, I felt the mattress welcome me. Perhaps five minutes had passed. My two cats were lying next to me, curled up in one large ball of warmth pushing against my left hip.

Without warning, I heard the sound of creaking floorboards in the hallway, as if someone were walking on them. Startled, because I live alone when my son is at his father's, I took a wary look toward the hallway. I saw nothing. Again, at the very threshold to my bedroom, I heard the creaking. Both cats sat upright, growling softly. Frightened and feeling vulnerable on my back, I shifted to a fetal position, facing the doorway. It was apparent there was no actual person; whatever was there was invisible to me.

I had questioned my mentor, Ellen, about this sort of thing a few months previously, wondering if I could be vulnerable to energies and beings that meant me harm. I was just learning to open to different realities.

"Remember you are always in charge," she had told me. "Keep something close to you that you value for its spiritual significance. Whether it is a crucifix or an amulet, whatever it is, it should be something that makes you feel safe. And when you do your meditations and readings, always remember to ask for assistance from the Beings of Light and Universal Brotherhood, and for all else to go back from whence it came. Then, if you feel something uncomfortable or feel threatened, simply tell it in a very firm voice to 'Go away!'"

Keeping these admonitions in mind, I bravely spoke up to whatever was in my doorway. "Go away! I'm not in the mood for this and I want you to leave!" The noise continued. More forcefully this time: "Go away! I will not be bothered! Now leave!" The sounds stopped as suddenly as they had begun. The cats remained sitting for a moment or two, apparently making sure that all was well, and settled back into slumber. They certainly were asleep much sooner than I, but eventually I did the same, though restlessly.

The following week, I mentioned my experience to Ellen in our weekly session. As usual, she was not surprised, remarking, "Maybe it was a guide trying to get in touch with you. Have you tried autowriting?"

At this point in my spiritual education I was still very much the cynic and skeptic. "Autowriting?" I replied, sarcastically. It was clear I didn't know what she meant, so patiently she explained. "In daylight, so it is not a vulnerable time, sit in meditation with a pad and pencil. Empty your mind and ask if there is a guide that is wanting to contact you. And if that is so, now is the time." I was skeptical, but more than willing to avoid another nighttime encounter.

Sitting in my living room the next day, I followed her instructions. To my complete amazement, the pencil in my hand began to move. It took some doing to give up control and allow whatever it was to take over. It became easier as we progressed.

He (no gender was specified, but I sensed a maleness) was Fernyl, my guardian angel. They are nameless where he is from, but names are a help to us humans. Fernyl is simply the name he wrote down so I had something to call him. He explained that he was present to help me with my purpose, just as I was there to help him with his.

"Good," he said, "Now we can begin. Let go. What I have to tell you is very important. You have to be more trusting of us. What I want to say is this: Go to where you are needed; do what you must do to make yourself heard, and you will be rewarded beyond belief. Not the kind of reward you think—much, much bigger. You *must* make them understand. The time is now to fix the world and we can help you do that."

My son called from the next room.

"Go see what he wants. I will wait. I'm always here anyway; you just have to ask. Go!"

Upon my return Fernyl continued. "Now you know who I am. You can open your eyes, but don't guide me. Okay?"

I began a question-and-answer format, speaking to him telepathically, while he answered on my paper.

I was confused about some of the things he had already told me so I asked: "Will you explain what you mean?" "Yes," came his penciled reply. "It will make you more attuned to Spirit if you have to work in a different brain wave." Some of the answers to my questions made sense only much later.

"Can I tell anyone?" I asked.

"Yes, anyone you like. We want everyone to know we are here."

I asked then if my son Morgan had a guardian angel.

"Of course," he replied, adding that I should encourage Morgan in the use of his guide.

In response to another question, he apologized for having frightened me. It was unintentional, he said, just that he tended to be a bit "heavy-footed." The Universe really does have a sense of humor!

My own particular Path, as many others who follow a spiritual life can attest, was unclear to me.

"Have I strayed from my Path?" I wanted to know.

"No, never off Path, just slower. The will is great. You don't know what we can communicate to you; you don't trust. The bigger story is not yet formed for you. You might find it in everyday life or activities. Yes, higher consciousness is the key. You need to focus more on us and the Great Plan."

"What can I do?"

"Do as you have already been instructed and spread the word. You must get Morgan to use his guide. Tell him his guide will help him more than anyone here in this realm can. He will help him with EVERYTHING. (The capital letters were his.) The boy is sensitive."

"Should I use the White Light meditation (for Morgan)?"

"Explain that meditation is simple, just necessary to connect. Do not be afraid. Be there with him. Yes, coax him if you must, he will see when he starts."

"What do you see for this Plan?" I asked.

"Greatness, hordes of angels, good beings, good deeds, lightness. But it is people like you that can help bring this to fruition." He seemed to sense my reluctance and my doubts that I could do such a thing. "Yes, a very BIG JOB. Yes, it will help you not to worry about it. If you really love and believe in you, you believe in us, etc., etc., etc."

"Can I foretell the future?"

"Long time, yes. You will get better. Yes, continue with Ellen. She has a debt to you and will impart much."

As long as I was asking, "How about aura work?"

"Not for you, long time. You work on visionary work." I guess I already knew that answer.

"Follow my Heart?"

"Always do that. *Heart* only! I want you to go to the store and talk for me, so . . . ." Again, my agitation and doubt were obvious to him. "Yes, too hard, don't try."

I attempted to apologize. It all seemed rather overwhelming if I were to literally do as he said.

"Yes, although good you heard me first. Specifics are such that you must let others know I have come to talk through you and they can ask questions. Yes, you are getting our clues, keep up the good work. Not to worry." (Yeah, don't worry, be happy!) "Good things come to those who wait." (I couldn't believe he was really saying this.) "Follow what you're doing. Learn much and you will see the way we want you to go. It will be new and yours alone. Not really new, but yours."

I made another reference to Morgan.

"Give him time. Yes, it's clear."

Anybody else to whom I should listen?

"Yes, Deedie will help you bring forth my voice. She will be reassuring. Yes, go rest now."

This was all very exciting, and at the same time I didn't feel like I had been given any real information. But as time has passed, and my trust in Spirit has grown to the point it is the number one thing in my life, many of the responses and admonitions from Fernyl during this first encounter have become clear.

For instance, when he said if I love me and believe in me, I love and believe in them as well. I have grown to know that God/Spirit resides in me fully, so of course we are One and the same. Therefore, if I trust me and believe in me, then I trust Spirit. Regarding the "reward" of which he spoke, I have already been rewarded by the ability to be in Divine Union with God in my healing work. To be an intermediary for those wanting a healing, or to feel a blessing from a loved one;

nothing on this earth compares with that experience. There have been many, many rewards besides this; more than I can recount here.

Morgan has done his own connecting and has spent time in meditation, receiving answers from other "heavy-footed" angels. Only recently have I come to understand Fernyl's instruction: "I want you to go to the store and talk for me . . . ." Jesus also spoke in parables and his meanings were not always transparent. For Fernyl, I could take him to the store in any form I wanted—even in the form of a book.

I believe we need a new language to tell an old story, a story as old and beautiful as creation itself. We have many directions to go with our story. It is far from complete; I don't believe it ever will be finished. Perhaps this is what he meant by "not really new, but yours," in reference to my Path.

We have to be patient when we get messages from the Universe. The answer will come when it is time. I was very private regarding the spiritual work I was doing at that time. Now I am willing to tell everyone and anyone who will listen, and have chosen writing as my best avenue of expression. Spirit doesn't care as long as the job gets done! We have assistants all around us; we just need to ask for their help. And yes, it is a BIG JOB! But I wouldn't trade it for anything in the world.

The Day I Knew

For years I'd been cynical and disbelieving of anything other than the material world. It was my culture, what I'd been taught and believed. Even when I began to do psychic readings, and knew things about people I preferred not to know, I remained somewhat a Doubting Thomas. Then my sister found a breast lump and everything changed.

It was March of 1996 and I had been working with Ellen Solart since the previous September. I had been spending time in meditation getting to know my inner self, learning how to trust my heart and the inner voice that guided me. I had practiced psychic readings on friends and had started a small business. The feedback I received was positive and I continued to explore through meditation what was in store for me in this new dimension.

My sister Janet had discovered a breast lump, and asked me to be in the doctor's office with her for the biopsy. She was anxious, but the doctor felt that an ultrasound examination indicated nothing to worry about. He proceeded with the biopsy on Tuesday and encouraged her to go ahead with her plans for a weekend in California. The results were due on Friday. Straightaway, I had two concerns. For one, I had a bad feeling about the breast lump, and believed she had cancer. Second, her husband was to follow her to California on Saturday, and she would be alone with a house full of children when she got the biopsy report. Trying not to alarm her, I asked her to call me after she heard from the doctor.

Friday came and went with no word from Janet. Waiting on pins and needles I finally called her myself late Saturday afternoon. She was very apologetic. The children had been a handful, Bill had just arrived and she had forgotten to call. "Oh, the biopsy was fine! They said there were some changes, but no cancer and not to worry." She was obviously relieved, and proceeded to enjoy her time off. I, on the other hand, was puzzled. My feeling hadn't changed and I wondered how I'd missed the mark.

Two months passed. The lump in my sister's breast continued to grow, and she was advised, even though it was benign, to have it removed. Arrangements were made, and I went to the surgical center with her to support her and be with her after the procedure.

Afterward, when the surgeon entered the waiting area, I knew immediately it was bad news. Cancerous tissue often has a distinctive feel to it; gritty, sometimes tough, fibrous, different than healthy tissue. The doctor hadn't found the good, healthy tissue he had expected surrounding the lump. The abnormal tissue was sent to the lab, and again we played the waiting game. I knew it would get worse before it got better. I told no one.

Within two days we had the truly bad news. My dear, only sister, did indeed have breast cancer. We are a close family and it hit us all very hard, especially her twin brother, Fred, himself a physician. He could comfort her, but couldn't rescue her. She already had the cancer; he couldn't prevent that. He had to sit by the sidelines while other doctors cared for her. They were pushing hard and fast for removal of the remaining tissue; the theory being that once you have cut where cancer is present, it is more likely to spread. Her choices were mastectomy or lumpectomy followed by radiation—a decision she had to make before her swirling head could thoroughly absorb the facts. A lumpectomy, with lymph node resection, was the option she chose.

The family went with her to the hospital in Phoenix, where the next procedure was to be done. I still knew it would get worse before it got better. And still, I told no one. My mother, father, brother-in-law and I all began the long wait. To offer support and encouragement, I had told Janet I would check in with her in meditation during her surgery. An hour or so passed and I spent some quiet time in the chapel in meditation with her. What I saw in my vision surprised me. The vision was a lymph node resection, in which the doctors dissect and remove the lymph nodes on the affected side and check for cancer. I had assumed the lumpectomy would be done first. It was as though I were right there in the operating room.

I had been an operating room nurse in the past, and I marveled at the reality as I looked at the tissues and muscles, open as if in a medical textbook. Everything I saw seemed absolutely tangible.

Switching gears, I let Janet know I was with her, reassured her and rejoined my family upstairs. We continued to wait. Finally, three hours into what had been scheduled as a two and one-half hour surgery, we received a call from the surgeon.

"We are just finishing the lymph node resection; it took longer than we anticipated. Now we're moving on to the lumpectomy," she told us. The others listened intently; I pondered my experience in the chapel. My vision had been correct. They had done the node resection first. How did I know?

More time passed, and I felt a sudden agitation spread over me; I knew it concerned Janet. As quickly as I could, I made excuses to the others, and found a quiet corner where I could be by myself and reassure Janet in my mind.

"It's okay, Janet," I told her silently, "You're almost done; it won't be long now." Janet had taken good care of herself for years. She ate well, was a runner, took her vitamins religiously, and did not run to the doctor without good reason. It had been very difficult for her to accept the need for medical intervention, and she was especially frightened of the anesthesia.

She was still under anesthesia as I spoke with her telepathically. I spent at least ten minutes trying to calm her. She was adamant in her struggle. "I want to go! I'm tired! I'm done! I just want to be done with this!"

"No!" I countered. "Just a little more . . . they're almost finished, and then you will be back with us!"

It was quite a struggle. She really wanted to leave. Leave to go where, I'm not entirely sure. But it was like holding her down on a bed when she really wanted to rise. She is my older sister, bigger and stronger than I. If she meant leaving her body . . . and dying . . . I wasn't about to let her do that. Finally calming down, she seemed to drift into sleep.

Again, I had a vision of the surgery. This time the incision was closed, and a gloved hand kept blotting the incision line, where a bit of blood oozed from the wound. I watched, fascinated, recognizing the type of surgical towel that was used to stop the bleeding. Then the vision faded.

After four hours, the surgery was finished and the doctor came to speak with us. More bad news. They had not been able to get clean margins. Clean margins are good, healthy tissue surrounding the cancerous area. Janet would now need a mastectomy. This is what I had anticipated all along, never speaking of it to others. I was not at all surprised; everyone else was in shock.

As the surgeon explained the difficulties she had encountered, I began to appreciate the clarity of my visions. As she turned to leave, she added one caveat: "Be sure to remind Janet not to take any aspirin before the next surgery."

I knew she had not taken any aspirin, and explained this to the surgeon. Janet had complained the night before of a headache, unrelieved by Tylenol. My sister preferred aspirin, but knew she couldn't take it before the surgery. "Well," the surgeon responded doubtfully. "We had such a hard time getting the bleeding stopped."

My vision of the oozing incision smacked me in the face. Any doubts I had in the past, of my perceptions of this other reality, that which others cannot or will not see, were gone. Not only could I see things others could not, but I realized I had a responsibility to speak up when the situation called for it, and not keep my "hunches" to myself. They were not hunches; they were fact.

With new assertiveness, I flew into action, informing my family how we were going to care for Janet, and what we would and would not allow her to do. I knew she would try to make all this okay for everyone else, and I knew intuitively my big sister was in for a big transformation. How did I know? I didn't care *how* I knew; I just knew *what* I knew, and I would never doubt it again. Too much depended on it.

March 28, 2003

Janet continues to do well and is cancer free. Some may say she is "considered" cancer free. I know better. She *is* cancer free and I believe she will stay that way. I love her beyond measure and look forward to having her in my life for many, many years to come.

Playing With Auras

Dear Waiki,

Many of my early spiritual experiences were exciting but puzzling. I didn't ponder them too much, I just moved forward with trust. Looking back now, I realize they were a way to familiarize me with non-ordinary realities. I trust you will enjoy the following.

April 1996

I met a new guide today; her name is Velma. She showed up while I was in meditation. I had asked for any information that might be useful. That is often my approach to meditating; letting the Universe share with me what it will.

Velma said she was here to teach me about the softest and kindest aspects of the feminine spirit and soul in human form. She chose her own name because she wanted to be identified with an older, sweeter time. Velma was with me, she told me, to help me know what Love and kindness actually felt like, in a palpable sense.

First, she let me feel her aura. It was curvy, wavy and delicate with much freedom of movement. You may wonder what an aura feels like. While I conversed telepathically with her, it was as if an unseen presence took my hands, and they suddenly felt much lighter than usual. I felt resistance between them, much like holding the positive poles of two magnets together. It was energy! Right there between my hands and arms. Quietly she faded away, as my spirit friend Mort made his presence known.

Now, Mort is another matter. I've had Mort in my life as a spirit guide since I was 17. Both he and Fernyl, my guardian angel, told me of Mort's purpose. He prepared me for other aspects of Spirit, so I would accept them and not be frightened. Mort is always available to me and he, too, let me feel his aura today. It was very different—strong and linear, but with a tendency to expand. He told me that he was a form of masculine energy, sent to help me with my strength, my trust in myself, and strength of being. How incredibly fortunate I am to have so many beings in this life to help me toward my purpose!

This was a day of many surprises, and now, for the best of all. I found my head being turned toward the left, where Fernyl had appeared. Fernyl asked me to open my eyes and look at him. That proved to be exceedingly difficult. All I saw was a brilliantly white image. I had to close my eyes quickly; they watered so much from the intense radiance. Then he let me feel *his* aura. It was enormous! I knew I was feeling only a very small aspect of him; the aura had no shape, only expansion. I shook from the intensity of it, but still felt privileged to be allowed to feel just a portion of what he is about.

What a morning! I took a long nap after that. Playing with such energy is joyful, but it is also tiring.

The Angels Speak to Morgan

Dearest Waiki,

As you know, Morgan is an enormous part of my life, and one of my best teachers. In this instance, he showed me how being fearless and trusting in a most unusual situation brought him—and me—illumination and fulfillment.

April 1996

I was becoming accustomed to the strange comings and goings of Spirit. In the last seven months alone, I had experienced a communication via autowriting with my guardian angel, verified the purpose of the guide who had been with me since I was 17, and not only had I met two more guides, but I had also felt their auras. It was becoming a full house! But the house was to experience a greater fullness yet.

It was after nine at night, and my son Morgan had gone to bed. Sitting on my couch in the living room, I felt the evening's quiet settle around me. As I relaxed and centered my breathing for meditation, my awareness heightened, and I entered that particular state of tranquility and calm.

Lost in the reverie of the breath, I breathed deeply, and became aware of a creaking sound coming from my left. It was the gentle creaking of the floorboards, and the noise came and went. There seemed to be a progression of the sound, from left to right, with other creaks filling in the gaps. In the space of ten minutes, in an area that spanned 15 feet, it was as if a symphony was playing in my living room, albeit a symphony confined to the notes of old floorboards!

This time, there was no need to inquire as to the nature of the sound. The brightness that shone through my eyelids, and the gaiety I felt in the room, spoke for the angels. It was apparent, in that special way of knowing, that these were heavy-footed angels, come to join me for an evening of quiet. I was the only one being quiet, though.

Unexpectedly, Morgan came out of his room, rubbing his eyes and complaining of the inability to sleep. "I don't know what it is, Mom, there's just a really weird feeling and I can't sleep. I'm kinda scared." I chuckled under my breath, and with my eyes still closed replied, "Well, I'm not surprised, although its nothing to be scared of. There are quite a few angels here in the room, and they're making a bit of noise." Without so much as a *really?* he excitedly plopped down on the couch next to me and said, "Would you ask them if I would be happier at a different school? If I changed schools, would things be better for me?"

Morgan was in eighth grade at a local, private school. He had been having trouble with a boy in his small class of thirteen; the boy was bullying him constantly. My mentor Ellen and I had given him positive ways to deal with the problem through visualization, walking away, and other nonviolent means. I've always felt it best to let kids work these challenges out for themselves; so far there had been nothing physical, but plenty of scare tactics. To make matters worse, the boy had convinced most of the other boys to give Morgan the cold shoulder, too. Here was this beautiful, sensitive soul, blossoming right in front of my eyes, yet his schooltime hours were misery. We had talked of other options, but there were only six weeks of school left and I was reluctant to move him.

At this juncture of my learning, I had little experience talking with angels, and to essentially be a conduit for their responses to my son's questions was a little awe inspiring to say the least. I told Morgan I wasn't sure it was appropriate to ask angels that sort of thing, but after much begging on his part, I figured they could always say "No."

So I asked. Of course, being angels, they had already heard Morgan's question and responded just as I was beginning to form the original question in my mind. "It is best if he learns to follow his heart and make his own decisions." The feeling I received was kind, but firm. I translated this to Morgan. Morgan was determined.

"Please? I just need to know if I'll be happier and do better if I'm at a different school. Please? Won't they tell me?"

Again, the same response from our angelic community. Morgan was more adamant, and his voice quivered with emotion. There was a brief silence on the other end, then with something that sounded like a sigh, they responded.

"We don't generally give this type of information, and reiterate the need to find your own answers. But this one time we will answer you. Yes, you will do better and be happier if you change schools." End of discussion. Morgan gave thanks.

That settled our dilemma. With a leap of joy and excitement dancing in his eyes, Morgan bounced off to bed and was asleep in record time. I sat quietly, content to be in the warmth and illumination, both inner and outer, of what these beautiful beings had given us.

Two weeks later, Morgan counted fifty friends at his new school. He was welcomed with open arms, and his studies improved. Angels don't lie.

The Sacred Dwelling Place of Man

Dear Waiki,

It had been a year and a half since Ellen and I began working together. I would check in with her periodically to discuss new occurrences or receive some guidance if I was unsure about the direction I seemed to be going. There was a change in the psychic readings I gave; a different voice that seemed to project from deep within me. It had been apparent to me for some time that the psychic readings were simply a means to an end, a way to practice reliance on my intuition, my inner voice, and letting Spirit speak fully.

On a particularly pleasant, sunny day as I sat in meditation, two new guides made their presence known. Seated comfortably in my cushy, oversized chair, I must look like Lily Tomlin in her "Edith" role; as a petite woman, I'm enveloped by the chair. That, of course, is why I like it.

Soon after entering a relaxed state, I began to experience a peculiar feeling in my throat, signaling a voice other than my own. Similar to beginning a psychic reading, my back straightened and my posture was more at attention—all the signs of Spirit. I began to speak in a low, guttural language, unfamiliar to me. There were clicks and a deep, grating aspect to the voice. Somewhat monotonous, it had a rich and resonant vernacular; at the same time it was rough. As my hands flew along with the words, it became apparent that two voices were speaking. Initially, they spoke to each other. Then, as I began to understand in a telepathic sense what they were saying, they spoke directly to me. The unusual language continued, reminding me of Native American speech I have heard.

At this point in my life, I was concerned with large ecological issues only in a general way. Yes, I told my son not to let the water run, as we live in a desert region, and I did my share to recycle. But I did not drive an economical vehicle or actively participate in any social movements. Although I was comfortable being in Nature, my connection to the earth had not developed, therefore it was clear to me this unusual message was not coming from any aspect of my personality.

The two beings that occupied my room were very different from each other. The one on the left seemed large in presence, and had a masculine feel to him. The spirit on the right was smaller, with a feminine quality, yet she was more demanding that I understood their intent and concern for our world. Indeed, that was the nature of their visit. They came to let us know that we, as a species, were headed for an unpleasant end if we continued our consuming, populating, and dominating use of this planet.

Their planet, they told me, was now black and dead. They had destroyed it in much the same manner as the human race seemed to be headed. In addition, they said, there were "volumes and volumes" of books they could share that held the knowledge of how their world had been destroyed. Through language, telepathic connection and hand movements, they told me how concerned they were, and that they wanted to help us. It was made eminently clear they especially wanted to provide help "for the children." This was done with an elegant downward sweep, signifying a smaller person, someone incapable of self-care, left to the whims of a larger, controlling group of people—us.

The two entities kept repeating one particular word I remembered for some time afterward; the only word I could put to memory, so unusual was the language. The word seemed to have particular significance as they came back to it repeatedly. The word was *mon'qua*.

After conversing for some time, I felt I was in vital communication and had a deep understanding of these two beings. I wanted to continue, so I could hear of the books they spoke of. But that was not to be. We had been talking for 40 minutes. They emphasized it was time for them to break the connection, as I was growing tired. "No, no! I'm fine!" I attempted to reassure them. Gently, they assured me they would return when it was time, when I was better suited to a longer association. As abruptly as they appeared, they left. I fell into dreamless sleep for two hours.

I pondered my encounter, and in my excitement told a friend about it. Her reception was chilly. She feared I was getting involved in something evil, and said I would "get over this sort of thing." It was a good early warning that not all would understand. I didn't wonder why my visitors didn't speak English; it would become apparent when the time was right.

Then, in the Utah desert, two months later, I heard the Quechua language for the first time. It is the language of the Q'ero Indians of the high Andes. Startled, I listened intently to many of the words Don Américo shared with us, as he defined various aspects of existence, energetic cleaning and doorways of initiation. The language had a remarkable similarity to that spoken by my two guides. Later, through an interpreter, I asked Don Américo if the word *mon'qua* had any meaning to him, if there was a similar word in the Quechua language. Looking surprised, he said, indeed, that it meant "the sacred dwelling place of Man."

More and more, I loosened my hold on the physical world that insists that a coincidence is just that, and only what we can see is real.

Angel on the Highway

Angels are everywhere. You just have to know where to look. Miracles happen every day. We just need to learn how to recognize them. I have had the enormous pleasure of conversing with angels, feeling their presence, and once was invited to feel a small portion of my guardian angel's energy. Angels really are everywhere, including some that look like ordinary people.

On a damp, cold Saturday in late May 1996, I was driving home from Phoenix. Every year at this time I hosted a cantina party in my backyard. One of the advantages of home ownership, this particular party place came with the house. I had been out of town visiting a friend, and was anxious to get home to my guests.

While driving on the highway, I always check the gauges. My father instilled in me the knowledge that gauges are much more useful than "idiot lights" and I have learned to rely on them. A few miles after exiting the interstate, on a relatively quiet road, I glanced at the temperature gauge. To my horror, it had shot up to red in the last ten minutes, indicating an impending boil-over. Immediately, I pulled over and popped the hood. Steam was already coming from the radiator. Puzzled, I began to look things over, knowing that there were no previous problems with the radiator and that the car had been serviced recently.

Bent over the engine, I had not noticed the car that had pulled over 30 yards or so ahead of me. Then a man made his presence known, as he spoke in a calm, quiet voice. Still well away from me, he walked at an angle to my left, so I could see him clearly.

"Hi there, I didn't want to frighten you. If you'd like, I can come have a look at the engine for you. I'm a truck driver, and know my share about engines."

He suggested I could move away if I wished, rather than be close to him while he looked under the hood. As I did, I also took note of his height, hair color and build. He seemed truly concerned for my welfare; although on a lonely stretch of highway, I wasn't going to be taken in by anybody. With some distance between us, we discussed the problem. I had reached some tentative conclusions of my own, and when he mentioned the water pump, I figured he was right.

There would be no water pump repairs out here. I couldn't have my car towed to my regular mechanic; he was closed and his gate locked on Saturdays. In the nearest small town, not only would I have to find competent service, parts would have to be ordered as well. The list of hurdles went on. And there were my guests, due to arrive within the hour.

With his quiet voice and manner, and with non-threatening body language, the man suggested that he give me a ride as long as he was headed my way. While he waited patiently and silently, I took some time to think this over. He made the offer only once, and I felt no pressure. It was as though I had all the time in the world.

Finally, I secured my car, grabbed my suitcase and followed him to his little car—an older Japanese model, with various dents and scrapes in its blue paint. But the interior was clean and uncluttered. From his demeanor and his style of driving, I concluded that the dents and scrapes had been inflicted by someone else. We talked little on the 40-minute drive, but I discovered that he was married, had two small children and lived in the Prescott Valley area. I tried several times to get his name straight so I could send him a card of thanks. It was complicated, perhaps Polish, and it sounded different every time he repeated it.

As quietly and calmly as he had driven, he dropped me off at my doorstep. I tried once again to conquer his name, and again the pronunciation sounded different. Grateful, smiling and relieved to be home, I set down my suitcase and turned to wave. His car had already disappeared from view. A bit put off, with guests coming and things to do, I could only think "That's odd . . . ."

After calling the tow truck, I made a stab at finding my rescuer's name in the phone book. Looking for "Smolkenkowsky," or something akin to that, I figured there would be only one such name listed. I was wrong. There was nothing even close. "He's a truck driver, for pity's sake!" I muttered to myself. "He's got to have a phone." I found nothing; not in Prescott or Prescott Valley; not in Chino Valley, Mayer, Humboldt, Bagdad or any of the surrounding communities.

Playing over the afternoon in my mind, I rewound my mental video to see his every move and gesture, to listen to his voice, to notice how he handled everything, including his leave taking. Puzzled at first, I soon began to laugh. In a moment of insight, I realized: He was an angel. "You never know when an angel will show up!" I thought to myself. And you never know what they'll look like.

Pay attention out there as you walk through life. Angels can be anything from the man who saves your day to the homeless street person who blasts you with a nuclear smile just because you looked him in the eye and smiled first. And the miracles? You got up today, didn't you?

Humility

Dearest Waiki,

Standing with my spine pressed against a pine tree today, I fondly remembered one of my greatest teachings on humility. Smiling as I thought of you, I saw the scene as if it were yesterday.

In the dappled shade of a ring of cottonwoods, a group of 12 sat in a circle, mimicking the trees around us. It was our third day in the canyon wilderness of Utah, and I was astounded at the things I had heard and felt from objects I previously thought of as inanimate, such as stones and the wind. You taught us to perceive energy, to realize the cosmic filaments that connect us all, and how to utilize these realities for the benefit of ourselves and others. Always for others.

On this warm morning we sat in a circle to hear what you had to teach about humility. In the work of service, we must be humble, you told us. Gazing around, with half-closed eyes, I noticed a few people taking notes. "How can they do that?" I wondered. Caught in the sing-song of your Spanish, followed by the translation into English, the information entered my heart, bypassing my brain. In later years I would wish for those notes. Even now I close my eyes to hear your concerns for our time on this planet and the work of the Spirit.

You spoke so poetically, so earnestly, of the special need for humility. You always speak of peeling the onion, the onion of the ego. To be humble is to toss off the shackles of the ego, to recognize one's nonimportance, to be able to grow in compassion and beauty, to embrace the significance of the whole as opposed to the importance of the individual. We are taught to accumulate personal power in our culture; this is what we must peel away, the importance of being special, that which makes us prideful, arrogant, slothful or unkind.

There are other manifestations of ego, so tricky it is. Maybe we were treated roughly, either as children or by loved ones. Maybe we have certain needs of diet or medicine. Whatever they may be, we must always remember to put aside our concept of difference. We must know we are the same as the trees and the stones, the clouds and the wind that scutter overhead in the deep, blue, Southwest sky. All of this, in its own beauty, is as unimportant as the shoes on our feet. Being humble in this way allows us to see the Cosmos in a different light. We are able to see our connectedness with the whole, and that perfection makes us important indeed. It's the ultimate paradox. I hope I do your teachings justice, Waiki. The words are mine; the energy and awakening of my own wisdom, that was your doing. You remind us "there is nothing new under the sun." These are not your wisdoms; you were brought here to unteach us, to reconnect us with that which we already know.

After listening to your instructions, I climbed to a conference with a gnarled, old juniper on the hill that had called to me with determination. "Listen to the tree," you advised. "Learn what it has to tell you." The tree had much to tell me; admonishing me in a kind, gentle voice. "Where do you think the wind comes from, that which you cherish so much?" it asks, with a bit of incredulity. For years I have noticed that when a solution to a dilemma presented itself or the "Aha!" to a silent, spiritual query was reached, a gentle wind from the southwest would always arise, reassurance I was on the right track. Simply grateful for the encouragement, I never thought of the source. Humbly apologizing, I felt the wind rise and move past me, grateful to All that make my Path sacred and possible.

Moving back down the hill to our circle of trees, I marveled at the knowledge I was gaining through Nature. As I entered the circle, I felt somewhat sorry for the others. No one else seemed to hear the voices I heard; their previous experiences seemed minor to the glories I had been having. I had a tendency to jump in with my newest development, so containing my excitement, I allowed others to speak first. My smugness soon faded to embarrassment, then to humiliation, lastly to dread. There was not a soul in the group who had not had some remarkable, sage wisdom from their tree. The energy of the circle leaped all around me as I realized what my lesson was. What was our subject that very morning? Talk about humility! In silence, I looked at my toes as I listened to each person recount their experience. If the lesson was to be complete, I knew I could not leave the circle without revealing myself wholly.

With utmost humility, I recounted my experience with the tree, mentioning the need to be grateful for all of Nature and its offerings. Then came the hardest part.

"In our lesson of humility, I have learned a great one, indeed. I felt that I was special because I could hear things that no one else seemed to experience." I felt as though I had been caught red-handed. "I even felt sorry for all of you because you couldn't hear these things. Now I sit here, completely humbled, and my lesson in humility is having to relate this special lesson out loud."

I finished. I sat in silence, knowing I had crossed a threshold and not to be proud of it.

You, Waiki, who see into people's hearts, needed no translation. You simply smiled.

The Face of God

Dear Waiki,

While first working with you in Utah in 1997, some of the meditations were so profound I was unable to write about them at the time. Time has not altered my experience or the understanding I gained that day. When we choose to put aside our mental dialogue and cultural teachings, the true glories of heaven and earth are revealed.

We sat as a group in the shade of the cedar trees. Américo was discussing the need to "remove the mind"; to put "the mind in service to the heart." I nodded, lost in reverie of the concept. Gisella, a native of Germany, vociferously argued, "No! I don't believe that! The mind is a good thing! We need it!"

Amused as always at the attempts of ego, Américo explained that of course, we do need it. It's just that the mind gets in the way, attempting to convince us of this or that reality. Primarily, the mind is too rational; western culture has trained it that way. So our meditation that afternoon was to let go of the mind, to let our consciousness go where it would.

Many times in meditation there in the desert, I had felt Américo create a specific energy for the group. Before we actually met, in meditation at home and on the drive to Utah, I felt Américo's energy, drawing me like an invisible chord. It was a soothing, palpable, Cosmic invitation to the unknown. That day in particular, I felt it strongly as he sat across a small gully from me, everyone else having left the vicinity in search of special spots for their meditation. Ordinarily, I would have left, too, but on this day I just settled into my chair and focused my intent to let go of my mind.

It seemed a short while before I lost all sense of my body, although somehow I was aware of a few ants making their way across my knees.

In meditation, I saw my body as a stone statue, white in the bright sun, ants wandering to and fro with no regard for me. I sat unperturbed, unconcerned about my surroundings. In front of me a river flowed, smoothly and quietly, full of multicolored rose petals. I rose and embarked downstream on a wooden boat. The stream twisted and turned in the canyons, past beautiful sandstone walls reminiscent of the Southwest, while I sat in complete rapture and wonder. After passing one bend, it ended abruptly in a box canyon, tossing me from the boat into piles of flower petals. Overcome by panic, "I'll drown!" I thought, and I began to claw my way upward. Just as quickly I told myself, "I can't drown in rose petals!" Instantly I relaxed, and began to swim upstream, my skin caressed by the velvety petals. They were cool and soft, and I laughed at the delight of swimming in a river of roses.

The scene changed again as I returned to my meditation spot. Seated once more, with tall, steep, snow-topped mountains to my left, I heard a voice call to me. Nervously, I avoided looking toward the voice. Uncertain how I knew, I was aware it was God, asking me to look upon His face.

"I can't look at God!" I said to myself. I was certain I would die, I knew myself unworthy, I was sure I would be blinded . . . a thousand more reasons zipped through my consciousness, all powered by my Catholic upbringing and by Western culture. Finally, I could deny the Power no longer. My eyes slid toward the mountains and gazed upon His countenance. And gaze I did. In amazed rapture, I saw a face white against the lower, green aspect of the mountainside, changing as I looked, showing me He was just a face, a face that could take on any particular appearance, just so I would feel right about the experience. It was a smiling face. Tears of joy coursed down my cheeks as I sat wrapped in utter wonder and glory. I didn't die, I was still here. And the best part of all, we, God and I, simply sat and smiled at each other.

From far away, I heard Américo's whistle, a signal to conclude the meditation. It was, and still is, the meditation most difficult for me to leave. With great reluctance, I stumbled down to the rest of the group, unable to share my experience. Not until much later did I feel myself fully back in my body.

I was shown a great beauty that day, by leaving my rational mind at home. And an added benefit of my experience with God, is that God and I smile at each other now, whenever we want. And far from dying, we revel in the wonder of *each other*.

Jaguar Coupling

My Waiki,

This is a meditation I want to tell you about, Waiki, one that took place in the summer of 1997, before my first trip to Perú. It was a puzzling meditation, but Tom gave me some insight, and I have discovered many implications since.

In my meditation, I am walking in the jungle. Tall trees of many varieties soar to the sky. Red and yellow flowers match the loud birds that take flight as I move along the narrow path. I glance down at my body, which is my own but muscled and brown. I am wearing only a liana tie around my waist. My breathing is nervous as unfamiliar noises abound. There is the racket of monkeys. A large, unidentified snake slithers away from me. Then, the animal that has been making crackling noises in the bush behind me, sounds that have been sending shivers up my spine, appears on my left. It is a large, heavily muscled jaguar, yellow with spots of black, so tall that I can touch his shoulder easily.

I am somewhat frightened, but as we walk in the rain forest, my fear subsides. It is clear that he means me no harm. We converse intermittently, but primarily it is a telepathic connection. We come to a small clearing in the path. I sit on the soft grass as the jaguar lies down with his mouth open for my inspection. Looking into his enormous mouth, at the large, yellowed teeth, I see the red, swollen gum surrounding a molar. Reminded of Androcles and the Lion, I remove the abscessed tooth, and he is grateful.

Then, without warning, I am on my knees and we couple. It is ecstatic, wild and passionate. I feel his hot breath in my right ear, I smell the foulness of the infection, I feel the great heaviness of his large, cat's body behind and on top of me. Watching in fascination, I am wide awake, meditating in my little room, watching as if it's a movie, a movie that feels completely real.

Then we lie resting in the clearing, and I am enveloped in his immenseness, cuddled in his embrace. A long period of time passes quickly and I am pregnant, giving birth to twins. The great jaguar never leaves my side. One twin is a human girl, the other a male jaguar. The jaguar leaves me to return to the forest, and I weep for him. He tells me I must return to my people alone, as he would frighten them.

Returning to the village with my children, I tell them the prophecy the jaguar has told me. These are both the children of the world, he said, and we must make a safe haven for them. We must treat them as equals in the world, and it is our job to spread the word. The men take long dugout canoes to the river's edge, put them in the water, and leave in groups. Some travel upriver and some downriver, to spread the prophecy.

What can this possibly mean? I ask Spirit. "Tell Tom and Bobbi,[6] they can explain."

A few weeks later, feeling embarrassed, I told Tom of my meditation, and that I was to ask for his assistance.

"This is about the bridge of the Q'ero,"[7] he told me. "They send out the energy of connection and Love. Some feel it; most don't. This is a bridge being formed for the work to be done. Rarely," Tom finished, "does someone like you, send it back."

By communicating with the Q'ero through the filaments of energy, I, too, was creating a bridge.

"The Work" is one of cosmic Love but set in the here and now. The Q'ero consider this the time of *pacha kuti*, the Great Transformation, a stepping out of time. This is the prophecy the jaguar spoke of. Mother Earth, *Pachamama*, is hurting. We are destroying ourselves as we destroy her. She will always prevail, but at what cost? The jaguar is but one creature that is an aspect of All; we must treat all of the *Pachamama* as One, to be handled with kindness and respect. The animals and other creatures on the planet aren't the only ones who will perish because of our folly. We, too, are linked vitally together.

You, Waiki, have commented that, "The more *salk'a* energy a person has, the easier it is to work with silence and with Magic. Then

6   Tom and Bobbi Best: mentors and teachers, owners of Blue Heron Productions, friends of Don Américo and the Q'ero.
7   Q'ero: Indians of the high Andes, direct descendants of the Inca.

the animals come to you, the wind caresses your face and the river sings to you . . . because you speak their language." In addition to connecting people through Love and energy, this meditation was a reminder of the vital connection of *salk'a*. *Salk'a* is wild, undomesticated energy that we all have within us, and it is our dynamic link to the Cosmos. The more *salk'a* energy we have, the more we understand Nature and the Cosmos. St. Francis must have had a lot of *salk'a*.

Spread the word, move the energy.

Initiation Into the Lloq'e

Dearest Américo,

You have spoken often of the importance of intent. Not intention, but intent. Doubtless, it was due to this teaching of yours that I was able to endure the hardship of this initial journey into the realm of the lloq'e, and thus learn of its tremendous beauty and bountiful mystery.

September 1997

This was my first trip to Perú. We were staying in Don Américo's home in the mountains, *Salk'a Wasi*.[8] Between ten o'clock in the morning and one o'clock in the afternoon, the house cleans itself energetically, so none of our group was allowed inside. There are those who live in the mountains and are simply cleaner than we are, so they were allowed to come and go. After a few days of visiting the temples in Cuzco, we had come to the mountains with the intent of getting our filaments clean. Then we would have a fiesta with the people of *Mollamarka*, the village that is adjacent to Don Américo's home.

We spent that first morning from ten to noon in meditation, and I meditated under a large eucalyptus tree, far from the rest of the group. My meditation that day, as every meditation that followed on that trip, was based on my intent of the *lloq'e*. In the Andean cosmovision, there is the *paña* and the *lloq'e*, the right and left sides respectively, in looking at the world and in terms of existence. The *paña* signifies the rational, knowable world, in which we reside. The *lloq'e* represents the mystery, that which we cannot know or understand. To use Carlos Castaneda's reference, it is the path of the *nagual* to walk effortlessly between both worlds. Since I had plenty of experience in the rational world, I felt I now should spend time in the *lloq'e*. This was the intent

8   Salk'a Wasi: Quechua for the House of Undomesticated Energy.

of this initiatory meditation. What I didn't know about the *lloq'e* is the absolute reality of that world, also.

Earlier in the trip I had a knowing that I wanted to clean myself "down to my bones." Always be careful what you ask for. As I sat in meditation, with my eyes closed, I had a vision of my naked body. There was a jaguar in front of me, and as he walked around to my back, I intuitively knew what was in store. Starting with my back, the jaguar clawed me to remove the skin from my body. It was astonishingly painful. The back was the worst, and I cried and wailed. These were real tears and real pain. It took a long time; time lost meaning for me.

Resting, catching my breath, I looked at my body. No longer covered with skin, now it was just muscle. Not some facsimile of a body, but mine: the contours of the legs, the feet, belly, these were mine. What now would be done about the muscles? Suddenly, fire! I burned, I howled! It hurt! Resting more, we had to get down to the bones. The jaguar studied me. I told myself many times during this process to be strong; I could do this. My only focus was the *lloq'e*. It was my mantra throughout.

As I watched in fascination, a strong wind began to blow the now-charred remains of my muscles from my bones. This continued down to the knees, and my mind wandered to "How am I going to share this meditation with the others?" It was a thought of self-importance. Suddenly a condor appeared, flew down, and latched on to my skull with his talons digging into my eye sockets. He began to rip and peck at the crown of my head, and I realized he was doing that to clean my energy channel, which runs from the crown down through the pelvic floor. This was the price of self-importance. I endured more horrific pain as he gripped his talons tighter. I cried out. I was strong, holding the vision of the beautiful children who now appeared on my left, the side of the *lloq'e*. There was one special little girl, whom I watched intently. She was the tiny, angel *waiki*[9] from Mollamarka, who came down to see our group on the first day.

My gaze shifted from the girl to the five jaguars who now appeared. They were all white, all sitting around me, observing the condor perched on my head. A white condor soared overhead to watch. Nearing the end of the condor's work on my skull, I felt each energy center of my body, each aspect of existence represented there—the *llankay*, the center of bodily power; the *munay*, the wisdom of the

9   waiki: (why'kee) an affectionate term, meaning brother or sister, in the Quechua language.

heart and Love; the *yachay*, the power and wisdom of the mind—all being cleaned, and I had only a paper thin piece left at the bottom of the channel.

The face of Don Américo appeared on my right as a representation of the rational world. It was clear I had to make a choice. To choose the work or hold on to my personal attachment to him and others. To truly do a work of Love, one must have unattached loving toward all beings, to be unconcerned about outcome. "No!" I shouted. "No quiero!"

The black condor took flight. "No, no . . . . " I begged. The children began to fade. I shoved Don Américo in the face with my hand. "No! No quiero!" I shouted. I wanted the children! I wanted the *lloq'e*! Suddenly Gáyle and Fernando, Américo's son and nephew, appeared on the right, and they all seemed to be laughing at me. I shoved them away. I was begging, pleading, weeping. I was in misery; I wanted the Work!

Instantly, the white condor swooped down through my channel and immediately all my bones and insides were brilliant white! Jaguars, children, *lloq'e*, it was all back!

I wept ecstatically. Now I could truly begin my Path. The words "Lo quiero, I love you" came to me, and for the next hour I loved everything that came into my awareness and vision. I sang these words to everything and everyone, dear and filthy, mud, feces, glorious children, my family and friends. I sang to poverty, crime, disease and beauty; it is all part of One, and it is all part of me. Such beauty I've never known. At last I was clean.

Two years after this experience, while in meditation, my guides told me I was a shaman who had been in training for years. After denying I could have such a background, I was instructed to "Go look it up" when I humbly asked, "Well, what is a shaman?" Yes, I had worked with Don Américo, but my need to understand, intellectual mind, didn't know all the things a shaman is or does. So I turned to the *Encyclopædia Britannica*. It was like reading my spiritual life story. Titles for a book to write swirled in my head, such as *The Reluctant Shaman*, but somebody had already used that title. Becoming a shaman is not something you just decide to do one day. It is something you are instinctively drawn to, or perhaps someone seeks you out. I began to read more and checked out every book my library had on the subject. It was as much to dispel the knowledge as to learn from it. In one of the many books I perused, I read about this very journey, as the author called it. It was an initiatory vision journey for a shaman-in-training. Although the animals were different, the context was identical to my experience. If the initiate survived, they were taken into training by the head shaman of the village.

To this day I do not call myself a shaman. In a culture where the shaman is revered and recognized to walk in many worlds, a shaman does not call himself a shaman. They are referred to that way by the rest of the community and sought out for their help. In addition, we are not an indigenous society; playing with titles can be ego-inducing. We must have a greater intent to be of service, as opposed to fluffing our egos with fancy monikers.

For me, it is a matter of not wanting to be pigeonholed. That feels confining and restricting. And in this work I want all the flexibility and wisdom I can attain. I am just at a small beginning.

Jungles and Jaguars

"You can't just *go* there!"

"That's the only way to do it—*go*. When there's a jungle waiting, you go through it and come out clean on the far side. Because if you struggle to back out, you get all snarled, and afterwards the jungle is still there, still waiting."[10]

The jungle had me now; I was trapped. Having lost my way, I was stuck on a small spit next to the river. All around me hung a thick canopy of vines that all looked the same. Determined to move forward through the ropy tangle, I climbed over and under branches, scratching my legs and arms. I knew there was a way out; I didn't want to retreat and backtrack. That was not in line with my intent. With focused obsession, I fought through the snag to my right. Within minutes, I was standing on a rocky shore, looking across the swift flowing waters of the Madre de Dios, a tributary to the mighty Amazon. Above me, blue sky mirrored the river like a snake, and emerald green jungle surrounded me on all sides. I was free and felt exhilarated as the energy coursed through my body.

This is meditating in the jungle. In the jungle you don't sit in quiet contemplation; it is a place for moving meditations. The jungle is always moving, so you move with her. You move to the sound of loud monkeys, the call and wingbeats of brightly colored birds, the soothing sound of the river, and if you're lucky, you move with stealth to the screech of the jaguar, who moves closer every time he calls for you.

So don't wait—*go*.

---

10   Matthiessen, Peter. *At Play in the Fields of the Lord*. NY: Random House, Inc., 1965.

The Warmth of Ritual

My Dear Américo,

My heart soars to know I will be with you and your family again very soon. To know we will traverse the mountains and valleys, sail through the salk'a *winds on the wings of cosmic Love, this warms my complete being. My memory drifts to another evening when I was warmed from the inside out.*

The night was cold and damp in your mountain home of *Salk'a Wasi*, as our group of intrepid, spiritual travelers prepared for ceremony to clean our physical and energetic bodies. It was necessary for our energy to be clean when we joined with the villagers in celebration. The wind blew outside, bringing with it a lashing rain. At 11,000 feet, one avoids the outdoors on a night such as this. Inside, by candlelight, we moved chairs and couches aside and laid down rugs, blankets, pillows and ponchos to soften and warm the ancient wooden floor. The house was also warm with the Love of the group; the extra layers of wool and polypropylene didn't hurt, either. You explained again the necessity of all the cleaning ceremonies, so we would be clean as possible to unite with the people of *Mollamarka* in a fiesta, planned for the next day. The people here live a life of simplicity, in union with the *Pachamama*, uncluttered by the frenetic pace of the industrial and technological world. In the mountains of Perú, Indians are always cleaning themselves and each other with the energy of the stars, the stones and the Cosmos. We were to engage in one such ceremony this evening. My soul has been touched by this particular ritual, the *Lloq'enacuy*.[11]

The shamanas, Doña Maria and Doña Feliciana, joined us as we settled in for the *Lloq'enacuy*, a new ritual for most of us. In the Andes, you explained, this particular ceremony is always done by the women shamanas. You were the assistant and very honored to be. As with all the ceremonies in which the Quechua people of the mountains

11   Lloq'enacuy: (yo ken a' qwee), cleaning ritual, performed by women shamanas of the Andes. See glossary.

engage, there was a *despacho*[12] made of certain objects the shamanas felt were appropriate. The contents of the offering can be made of coca leaves, rice, sugar, quinoa, a cookie or piece of bone, anything that comes from the shamana's own *despacho*,[13] combined in a small square of paper. These items were put into the *despacho* with great care, then burned and offered to the *Pachamama* before we began. We quietly visited and shared some beer and coca leaves. This was a solemn occasion, but a celebration, too. We were being cleaned and that is always a call for celebration.

You illustrate this beautiful ritual in your usual poetic way. The ritual itself is straightforward and, as you remind us, often subtle. For me, none of these cleanings are ever subtle. I guess I'm just wired for it. Yarn is wrapped around the left toe as the individual stands on five branches cut from a tree, placed in the shape of a star. Then it is wrapped up and around the knee, waist, heart, throat and forehead. The yarn symbolizes a feather, a feather that connects us to the *Pachamama* and the Cosmos. Starting at the crown and moving down, the yarn is broken at energy centers, one after the other. The *hucha* is released, leaving you clean and new again to the world. The other assistants in the ceremony include a runner, to hold the broken yarn with the *hucha*, and her guardian. When all the participants have been cleaned, the runner and her guardian sprint as fast as they can to the closest river, throw the *hucha* in the water, to be released to *Mama Cocha*,[14] who will finish the cleaning. The river in this case, is at least one-half mile distant, straight down. It is very humbling to know these kind people are so willing to do this work for us.

My memory of that evening in 1997 is one of soft light, quiet conversation, drifting in and out of meditation and the warmth of many old, internal fires. The warmth seemed to come from all of us waikis and from the colorful flowers you brought to the shamanas to honor their work. It came from the sense of safety from the guardian, who let us know our innocent, clean selves were secure from any out-side interference. It came from a place of mystery. The warmth is that same, boundless place where our spirits soar together when we fill the mountains with our laughter, and the place I always long for when I am not there. It is always available to me, this place out of time; being with you in the mountains simply makes it easier.

---

12   despacho: ceremonial offering.
13   despacho: dual meaning, collection of objects for ceremony.
14   Mama Cocha: the ocean.

All The Doors Are Open

My Dearest Waiki,

I write to you about a dream I had on my fortieth birthday. It was a quiet, reflective time for me. I had thought to have a large party with many friends, but was feeling reclusive and found myself with thoughts of death and rebirth, both literal and figurative.

September 1996

There were many water dreams last night. Many variations of going from place to place, swimming in pure, clear water, going from building to building via canals that connected a little city. It was a city of soft pastels, graceful arches, with an interconnecting system of canals on different levels, one above and below each other. Rather like a city of the future might look, the roads being canals full of water in which to travel. I swam naked, passing and waving to many people I knew. I was aware of my nakedness and not bothered by it. I swam languidly, not searching for anything in particular, just curious. But in my travels I found some passageways that simply ended in blind alleys and other passages I was not allowed to enter. There were many canals I could travel, as I slowly enjoyed my explorations. There were many men of Hispanic origin in this city, including one in particular I felt had a great significance to me. When I came to another area where I was not allowed to enter and was turned away, this same man came and showed me a different way to go. He said there were many other places I could go besides this. "Come, I will show you the way that is open to you."

Waiki, this dream was a full nine months before I started my work with you in Utah and we began our travels together. And when I re-read this journal entry, two years later, I discovered something interesting.

You were here in Prescott with your first camps, for the month of September, in 1996. Bobbi mentioned that you often came to people in their dreams.

That is not the end of the story, and some would write this off as a simple coincidence except for one more thing. At the end of my first journey to Perú, you, Tom and I sat talking of our work to come. In order to be certain you understood me fully, and with Tom translating, I told you I wished to join this work of Love and Beauty. I saw great numbers of people we would work with, large rooms of waikis to touch with the Sacredness of the Universe. In my enthusiasm, I envisioned a sizable center with fountains, with a city park close by, so people could experience the *Pachamama* even as they live in her concrete jungle. Maybe we could find a retreat center, close to a city with a lovely forest and water nearby, to reintroduce *la gente* to the wonders of the Mother. As always, you gave me your full attention and smiling, you spoke these words.

"I believe you, Waiki Marylin. I believe you can do anything you say you can do, and I have contemplated this three times.[15] I have made a decision. Because for you, life is different. For some, there are doors that are closed to them; some are open, some are closed. But you! All the doors are open to you, Waiki, and I will go with you and do as you say and we will do this work of Love. All the doors are open to you!" It took me two years to fully realize these words and their meaning. Waiki, thank you for paving the way and continuing to believe in me, especially in times when I didn't believe in myself.

---

15   Three times is Américo's method of making a decision.

Incan Morning Prayer

Machu Picchu, the glory of the lost Inca. Machu Picchu, the city that was re-discovered in 1928 by the famous archaeologist, Horace Bingham, founded for the glory of Western Civilization. People speak of magical energies there, the sacred power of the Inca, and the controversy over whether it was a sacred place of ritual, or a home to the ruling elite. My interest was primarily historical. I've been fascinated with everything Peruvian ever since my Grandma Maziebelle visited there when I was a child and brought me home a small stuffed llama as a gift. I had no expectations. I simply had seen many photos of the magnificent mountain that looks down upon this incredible stone edifice. I could not make a trip to Perú without seeing this mysterious place—rather like the pyramids, although to be completely honest, at the time, I had more interest in the pyramids.

That was my first trip to Perú, in September of 1997. The experience so far had been earth-shaking, mind-blowing and my life was now forever changed. Some journeys are like that. My experiences since meeting Don Américo Yábar and his mystical ways, only a few months previous, had been rather over the top. This aspect of our travels together was no exception. I was visiting Perú with a group of like-minded people, and together we were nearing the end of our travels. Now we would journey on without Américo; he had taken us to special places of learning, opening and meditation, but he doesn't go to Machu Picchu. I was soon to understand why. He did give us good advice about the ruins, a few places to meditate, told us not to get too close to the edge, and to journey home safely. Our stay in Aguas Calientes, the town at the base of Machu Picchu, was scheduled for three days.

We had quite a celebration our last night together with Américo before leaving. The train was early the next morning and we were feeling fragile from leaving our place of security in Américo's loving bubble, not to mention a bit too much *pisco*.[16] There were seven of us traveling to Machu Picchu. As the day continued and the landscape revealed the beauty of the Urubamba Valley, our spirits lifted as we began a new chapter of this Peruvian adventure.

Upon arriving in Aguas Calientes, we felt the familiarity of a small Peruvian town. We had passed through many such towns with Américo, and the sights, sounds, odors and small people with dark skin made us feel at home. Collapsing in our little room at the hostel, my roommate Linda and I got some needed rest. Later, we ventured out for dinner, looked around the town a bit, then returned to our room for more sleep and preparations for the following day.

We secured tickets for the bus trip up the hill. After an adventurous ride passing roaring rivers and encroaching jungle, with steep switchbacks weaving up the mountain, we were eventually deposited at the famous place of spiritual seekers and tourists alike, Machu Picchu.

What a shock! There were white people everywhere! While traveling with Américo, a native of Perú, the only white people we had seen in the last two weeks were each other. The Peruvian native is a quieter, more subdued person than the average American or European. What struck me initially about Machu Picchu was all the loud talk, the hordes of people milling around and the insensitivity to each other's personal space. That first day was spent primarily in meditation, watching the llamas munch grass, and attempting to adjust to a different kind of culture shock.

The next two days we acclimated and explored, meditated and strolled, and I peeked over the edge a number of times, making my roommate nervous. Américo had warned us of a descendant pull down the mountain if we were to venture too close to the edge, and being the constant skeptic and curious cat, I had to experiment. It really was an interesting phenomenon; there was a definite pull, and it took some force to pull back. Américo was not given to scare tactics; there was rarely conversation in his teachings about things that were bad or evil.

I grew up in a small town and have played, hiked and camped in many areas around my home. I am at ease in Nature. In recent years, as I have become more attuned to Spirit, it has been difficult for me to be around crowds for extended periods of time. At that moment,

16   pisco: cane alcohol of Perú.

on the afternoon of our last day, Machu Picchu simply had too many people, and I needed refuge. I found it, off the beaten track.

I was gazing down into the valley from a low wall, when I noticed a small, ill-used trail down to my left. Peering over the side, I could see a small opening in the wall below me. It looked like a cave. Looking over my shoulder to ensure I wasn't seen, I jumped the wall and headed for the cave. Like many of the places at Machu Picchu, this one had a reverential feel to it. I stepped slowly into the small space, which was intentionally cut into the stone face. It was about eight feet deep, eight feet wide and six feet tall. There were cutouts in the walls at the four directions: north, south, east and west. They looked as though they could have been windows; maybe they held candles in another time. On the north side was a stone bench, cut out of the rock. The ceiling sloped down toward the west, the direction of the rest of the temple. I explored all the nooks and crannies; it was damp and did not look like it got much traffic. There were pieces of burnt sage spread around, and a few other objects that might have been offerings: fragments of cloth, a stub of a candle, food items and the like. They had been there a very long time.

Sitting, relaxing, I felt a sense of deep peace in the cave. Quite at home, I meditated for a half-hour, until I felt a sudden but gentle pull to rise and stand. I turned toward the entrance, the east, as I felt a particular lightness in my body and arms. Bowing in respect, I began what felt like a dance with Spirit. Slowly, with great ease, my right arm rose like an eagle's wing, then began a descent as gracefully as a ballerina's as my left arm rose in opposition. I felt lighter than air. My arms and hands came together again in prayer position. I stood, bowed, and on one foot, spun in the opposite direction to greet the west. The movements were essentially the same at each direction, occasionally repeating a gesture for emphasis. I danced like flowing water. I went through this ritual four times, with my mind engaged, following the effortless movements, and aware of a language in my head that was now a bit more familiar, but still not translatable to me. It sounded very much like Quechua, the Indian language of the Andes, the ancient language of the Incas. I recognized it both from the bit Américo had shared in his teachings and from a meditation I had earlier that year. The meditation had involved two beings who spoke that language and wanted to warn us of the potential for doom of our planet if we continued on our destructive path. One thing that became clear in that little cave, was the gift I was offered: a prayer, to give thanks every morning to the four directions. Since then, in addition to the prayer of thanks to the directions, it has become a prayer of gratitude for the beauty and grace of walking this earth and the ability to move the energy of Love. I move that energy now, by offering you, dear reader, this prayer. Use it as you wish, with intent, beauty and Love. Dance it as I have, if you so desire.

The beauty of Machu Picchu and the gift I was given are with me always. I strive to see the beauty in all that others do, even when they're literally stepping on my toes. Please be mindful of how you impact the earth, this place we call Home. We need to learn to live in harmony with her, not subduing and polluting her, and I will do the same.

Don Martín's Favor

Dear Waiki,

With good-natured humor and a bit of exasperation, I have heard you tell a few individuals "I will cut off your head!" You have threatened this shamanic gesture when your students can't stop their internal dialogue, or continue to allow their egos to run their belief systems, thus disallowing them the possibility for a true heart opening. This technique fascinated me, as I waited impatiently for you to do this for one of our group. My ego didn't allow me to see how much I needed it.

What would it be like? Would all thought stop? How priceless! We are so bombarded with input, the sheer idea of no thought is difficult to comprehend. If it were me, where would my head go? Many questions arose as I pondered this process; not sure if it was symbolic or literal. As it turned out, you were not even present when my own head was cut off.

A cold, gray, wintry day in late 1997, I drove to Tom and Bobbi's house to do some work on the upcoming retreats. They had a beautiful home west of Prescott, in the mountains outside of town. It was an older subdivision, originally summer cabins that have now evolved to year-round homes. Theirs was an A-frame, complete with screened-in sleeping porch. The local ravens, javelina, squirrels and chipmunks were much loved and well fed there.

There was something I felt uneasy about that afternoon I could not identify. On one level, I felt as if I was holding back some deep, dark secret from my two friends. Unable to imagine what that might be, I also felt a peculiar, jangly feeling, as if I had drunk too much coffee. I attempted to concentrate on my tasks. After 45 minutes of this tremendously heightened, anxious feeling that came out of nowhere, I finally asked Tom for his assistance.

"Tom," I inquired with a worried tone, "I'm feeling really weird, like I've drunk a pot of coffee. I feel terribly anxious and it seems to be increasing. I have no reason to feel this way. I can't ignore it any longer; is there anything you can think of to help?"

Tom instructed me to sit in the living room and went about trying to find something. He asked his wife, Bobbi, if she had seen a particular stone he had in mind. She claimed she had not. Up and down the stairs he went, at one point poking his head over the railing and inquiring "Whose help do you feel you need most? Don Martín's or Américo's?" With eyes closed and focusing my energy to relax, I contemplated this for a moment. "Both!" was my reply. He muttered something about me being greedy as he came down the stairs.

Tom was unable to find the particular stone he was searching for and put in my one hand a triangular rock with a hole in it. "Martín himself gave this to me. It is a very powerful stone; I call it my vision stone." In my other hand he gave me a smooth, black stone he had received from Américo. In addition to the stones, he handed me a small pile of shiny, gold papers, each of them 3"x 3" square. Tom had returned recently from France where he had done an NLP (neuro-linguistic programming[17]) training. "The Frenchies have so much inner dialogue, that every morning before we began, I instructed them to place all their thoughts into these little papers, so they could start with an open mind, free and uncluttered. I told them when I returned to Arizona I would bury them with ceremony. I actually forgot I'd said that until I was leaving and they all said 'Wait! What about our papers!' They very much wanted me to bury these—they are very heavy (with *hucha*)."

Tom further explained: "Now, your task is this: In the training of a shaman, the elder shaman will have a task to do, a healing or something. He then gives the job to the shaman he is training, thus continuing to look good in the community but not doing the work!" He said this with a wry look in his eye and his ever present chuckle. Obviously this is how a shaman learns. "So, here you go," he said with a stern voice as he handed me the bundle of foil, "Go take care of the *hucha*." He gave me a few more instructions about intent and how much the French people were counting on me doing it right, and sent me out the door.

The wind had risen and the temperature had dropped since my arrival. The sky threatened snow. In a semi-trance I set out to perform the ceremony. I spotted the tree I knew would be right and in no

17   NLP: neuro-linguistic programming. See glossary.

particular hurry headed toward it. Bobbi's large, gray cat followed at a respectful distance. Upon reaching the tree I sat and meditated for some time. When I felt it was the proper time, I dug a deep hole at the base of the oak tree and solemnly buried the papers. Saying some words over them, I asked *Pachamama* to take them, clean them and give them back to the earth, ensuring the French people were kept clean by the process. Max, the cat, kept a close eye.

The papers buried, I sat on top of them with my back to the tree, and returned to a trance-like state. It felt as if I had known all along what would happen and who would perform the ceremony. Calmly, still in meditation, I waited and watched Don Martín[18] come from behind the tree, stand in front of me and very swiftly, lopped off my head. Fascinated, I watched the trees spin past me, as my head, disengaged from my body, moved away and to the south, 100 feet behind me. My head spun slowly and gently and then landed in a hole, eyes facing the gray sky. I had little time to wonder what was to happen next before the first shovelful of dirt landed directly in my eyes. Blinking hard, I quickly shut them before more dirt was shoveled in. Very shortly, in peace and contentment, my head lay in the hole, covered with dirt, while my body sat upright at the tree. There was awareness that the temperature had dipped more, but no sense of cold. Awareness of a deep quiet in the forest; I heard no sound. I was conscious of a deep calm, but no thought to go with it. An indescribable silence and serenity settled over me.

Much later, Max, my trusty guardian, nuzzled me and let me know it was time to re-enter present time and space. We walked quietly back to the house and I am forever grateful to know what it is like to experience being truly empty-headed.

I never did ask Tom what my feelings had to do with the papers. I suspect I simply had a lot of internal dialogue myself and upon entering the house, felt the noise from the Frenchies. When I returned to the house after burying the foil papers, there was such a inner calm that it never occurred to me to ask. I was grateful and honored to have performed my first real ceremony and have a ceremony performed for me. Life was good.

---

18   Don Martín: a kuraq akulleq. See glossary. Although I've never met him, I have a strong connection with this paq'o.

Letter to Waiki

My Dearest Waiki,

You have shown honor and respect for my being and have showered me with the beautiful poetry of the Love of the Cosmos. It is with great pleasure and ayni[19] I give you back the poetry of my spirit.

April 1998

Mi gran amigo, Waiki Don Américo Yábar, the gift of the light of your being is radiated off the luminous clouds of a summer day and the crystalline brightness of a cold, dark winter's night. The Love that emanates from your heart touches the mountaintops, the fish running upstream upon the stones and the hearts and bodies of countless children, both young and old. You are as old as the molten lava that runs beneath our feet and as young as the small twinkling light in the sky that is just reaching our earth some 20 million light years later. Contradictions, enigmas; you are too many to count. Being millions of mirrors for all of us to see ourselves in and to serve humanity, you lay yourself open to the energy of the Cosmos that we all may learn.

Like a hummingbird that flies thousands of miles without a map, the wind that is yours carries over those similar miles to create a bridge of three-dimensional feelings. This is done to reunite the peoples and spirits that alight on this earth so we all may go to the same place of Love.

For this beauty that you do, I in turn honor and respect you, and with much pleasure, join you in your work as it is my work also, mine being a bridge of Love. This, I vow with my word of energetic spirit, is what you can always expect from me: to feed you in your work and play with my energy of the cleanest, brightest light of the Cosmos. To

---

19   ayni: reciprocity.

clean you with my light, to shower you with the stars upon which you eat, to move the luminous, watery filaments toward you, that you may bathe in the river of Light in which you live and to always look forward to our many travels and the good wine along the way. This and much more we will share as I begin truly my work of Love. Once touched by the light, it radiates in me as the warmth of a thousand fires have warmed me in the past. It glows brilliantly and electrically from a tranquil, quiet center of pulsating orbs. It is always with me and I vow to stand always in the Light, speak from the Light and to be the Light.

You are the body incarnate in this lifetime that I have chosen to follow and work with, to feed and be fed by in the work of the Spirit, as we go toward transcendence and always back to the Light by going nowhere and doing nothing. Ask of me what you will, because I know I may do the same.

Hasta en los filamentos and give all of the above to your family and all the waikis of the mountains, jungle and stars.

Tu gran amiga,
Marylin

Maritza of Paucartambo

Dear Waiki,

What follows is the tale of your niece, beautiful Maritza, and our time together. I continue to be in awe of this wise, young woman, and in gratitude for her simple, yet elegant teaching.

Maritza of Paucartambo silently watches the wind swirl the dust in the streets. She, so light of feet, knows she can twirl much faster. Shyly, the young woman climbs into the truck with head down, excitement showing in her eyes. Does anyone else see it? Gáyle speaks to her, "Hola! I'm your cousin! It is an honor to have you with us." Her face flushes. This appears to be too much, but oh, how she enjoys the attention!

Beautiful young lady, going to the big city of Cuzco for a visit with her aunt. So lithe. "We have to put meat on her bones," you say. "See, she is too skinny!" I notice with American joy, yes, she is thin, but in America, this would be just right. I have learned to appreciate my bit of extra fluff in this country of poverty and beauty. I'm glad she has joined our trio of adventurers back to Cuzco.

Quietly, on only a few occasions do we speak. I am shy with my Spanish, she shy with hers. We stop for a break, I need my *q'uyas*[20] from the back of the truck. I show her some of my favorites, the amethyst from my son always being shown off. She nods, no words, what is that look? "These Americans are crazy," it looks like. It is only later I realize it is a look that a mother would give to a child, thinking, "So simple in her joy" or maybe "She's easily amused!" Yes, a look of a wise mother.

On the return trip from Cuzco she is with us again, this time on a bus with many Americans. Withdrawing further, speaking only when spoken to and then very little. Two hours out of Paucartambo you put

20   q'uya: a special stone with which you have a personal relationship.

us together, telling us both to get to know each other. A little awkward perhaps, but she is such sweetness. You knew I was looking for a reason to talk with her, but in my own shyness didn't know how. Like a flower, she turns and opens all of herself to me. I am overwhelmed. Always I had wanted a little girl, I thank her for the energy of young girl love she has given me.

We discuss school, I tell her of my 15-year-old son in the States. My God, how many conversations he has helped me start with los jóvenes![21] She sits with me now on the bus, very happy to be in a circle of Love. "Tú vives en Paucartambo, qué te gusta el mejor?"[22] I ask in my always suspect Spanish. Without a thought, "El aire puro." The pure air. What would an American say if asked what they like best about their home? Too much, I'm sure. The pure air. It says so much and then so little.

We travel on. Already, I'm feeling like a maiden aunt. Maritza continues to open up; it is like watching a butterfly open and take flight. No longer shy, she touches my knee to point out a mountain of enormous power when the conversation has lulled. We stop at Las Machulas, home of the women of the moon of the very long ago past when there were two suns in the sky. We are to have a meditation by one of the little buildings. "Do you want to come meditate with me?" I inquire. "Si," she says, sticking to me like glue. I'm in love.

Sneaking a peek during our meditation, wondering what does a girl from here look like meditating? I was not prepared for what I saw. Radiating from her young face was the perpetual wisdom of a primitive soul. Serene in its countenance, at peace and completely one, with and within her surroundings. This whole universe is truly her home. What she and others like her can offer the people of this frenetic world, both young and old, is limitless. This is not about living simply and poorly. This is about living completely. In a way I have seen and am too young to understand.

---

21   los jóvenes: the young people.
22   "Tú vives en Paucartambo . . . ": "You live in Paucartambo, what do you like the most?"

Gáyle the Protector

My Waiki,

This writing is in honor of your son, my dear friend and brother. One of the most beautiful people I know, Gáyle and I have a bond between us that reaches far beyond the stars. Words do this connection no justice; what follows is just one afternoon on the planet.

Mercury in this time warp, jet black hair, eyes with the softness of a mother puma toward her young. Fleet of foot and feats of strength, this kind soul with the light of a thousand candles in his little finger is my friend. With honor the size of the Grand Canyon, he leans out into the stars at the same moment he reaches for your hand.

Equally at home in the congested city, the small villages of the high Andes, even in a kitchen, cooking for the amusing American. Moving sinuously about la cocina, without conscious awareness, he happily dances to the music of the boom box and his heart alike. He makes rice, he makes papas fritas, he makes Jell-O—all with equal aplomb, serenity and a dash of spice.

Gáyle as the protector; it is easy to envision him with a royal blue hat and plume, as he bends to tell me what an honor it is to be at my service. We move through the noisy streets, shrill horns from quick moving cars, reminding me pedestrians are but swirling dust in the streets and you'd better move faster than that. Constantly he is at my side, the street side, as I begin to relax to a different way of moving through the world. No longer do I need the façade of toughness that eats away at my soul. With my vigilant shadow, I begin to open to the irritating smell of diesel in my nostrils, at the same time adjusting my sense of space as many bodies bump against mine. I listen to the cacophony of a Third World city, while money exchangers hawk their wares, and English lessons blast from the loudspeaker outside a small market. And me? I'm loving it all, because it means I am back in my spiritual home, in Cuzco, Perú. Without concern for where I walk, I slip my arm in his to gaze at the unwashed children, smiles adorning their brown, Andean faces, eager to sell the gum and chocolate to feed their many brothers and sisters at home. With open heart, beaming face, I continue my stroll through the congested, lively streets with my protector always at my side. I have returned home, honored by my caring brother, with a loving saunter, just to exchange some money.

Letter to Gáyle

Mi hermano Gáyle,

This is written in English so I can speak best from my heart and I know you will understand the intent. Gáyle, it is most difficult to put into words what you mean to me. You told me it was an honor for you to be my guide and companion, but truly the honor was mine. It was such a pleasure for me to put myself fully in your charge; I was treated like a queen. In my life here, I take care of myself completely, and it is with much relief I allow you and your family to care for me when I am there in my other home. Please, give your friends Enrique and Fernando, a very large thank you from me.

Gáyle, my heart is full (lleno) always of my visit to Perú in March, and I look forward to working with you and with the young people. Also with Arilu, my time with her was much too short.

Please send with Américo your love to me and my son, Morgan, and I will be sending you pictures of *Salk'a Wasi*. It will be too long until we meet again, but we always have the filaments and the intent that brings us close together. We will do fine work together, I know, in the future with the young people and all the waikis. My work is your work. There is a saying in English: "You are an old soul"; "Tú eres un alma vieja"—éste es mi pensamiento para tí. Muy, muy, viejo.[23]

Por favor, una cosa más. Tell Arilu and Velquis none of this is possible without the women. Ojalá, you understand my letter. You understand my heart, that is what is important.

Con mucho cariño,
Marylin

---

23   éste es . . . muy viejo: this is my thought for you. Very, very old.

Characters Along the Way

Dear Waiki,
*   You know well these beautiful souls I write of, but some explanation is useful for the reader.*

⬛ Our amazing Miguelito, gardener extraordinaire of *Salk'a Wasi*. A *paq'o*[24] of the mountains, he was struck by lightning at a young age. He is somewhere between 89 and 111 years old. No one knows for sure. The saying "He has a twinkle in his eye," must have been written to describe Miguelito. Don't let it fool you.

Bobbi is Bobbi Best, of course. At the time of this writing, she and her husband, Tom Best, ran *Blue Heron Productions*, the vehicle through which I met Don Américo. An amazing woman of numerous talents, she previously offered retreats in Hana, Maui, for the *Visible Woman*, and now, as in the past, works with at-risk teens. She taught me life-expanding lessons, and we shared good wine on our travels. Never try to keep up with a woman of French ancestry.

Linda Moore was a friend made in Utah, a roommate in Perú, and then my roommate in Arizona, before Al came into my life. Linda has an enlightened sensibility toward the word "yummy." The people of Mollamarka call her "La mujer de la risa," the woman of the laughter; she is indeed that. I wish her well on her journey.

Marylin, that's me. I spell it that way because when the Peruvians say my name, it sounds like Maa-ree-leen.

And last, and most important in this grouping, is Tom. Tom Best, of *Blue Heron Productions* and a magician in his own right. A long-lost brother, he forced me to find a language of Spirit that I could live with. He also forced me to look at many aspects of life I found rather unpleasant, but that are necessary to be aware of, in order to hold strong to the Path of Spirit. Thank you.

24   paq'o: the appropriate term for a mystic, or shaman of the Andes.

Miguelito

Miguelito of the night, of the lightning, of the hot breath. Small in stature, it is a good thing because if this man was much bigger this world might be too small a place for him. Whether in his weather-worn clothes or his best vestments as the shaman he is, he is at peace in *el jardín* as he moves the earth slowly back and forth with his hoe. He hacks the grass down with one quick movement that makes you wonder if the grass simply consented to move aside for him. The flowers grow under his tutelage of ancient wisdom and communication that only species of *salk'a* can understand. But this is just a side note.

To know Miguelito is to kiss him. You might think to kiss a 108-year-old man with teeth full of coca and wandering hands might be a bit of a shock culturally. When you surrender to the intimate gesture that is offered, this is what you will find: The very breath of *Pachamama* herself. He is a living, breathing volcano. This man breathes fire into your body with every breath. Back and forth you tumble—in, out, the hot fiery breath continues. "Do you want to lay with me in the garden over there?" he inquires. "No, thanks, I think I'll just take my coffee and sit on the wall. Ciao, Miguelito, hasta pronto." He looks a bit sad, then smiling, readjusts the load of fire sticks he laid aside upon seeing me, and heads up the path.

Bobbi

The cat, never quite domesticated, is sleek in this one. In some former life (maybe in this one on moonless nights), this woman was not just any cat, but a Korat. The silvery tipped coat with the heart-shaped face and large green eyes are the hallmark of this rare breed. So it is with the woman. With eyes that catch you spellbound and hold you there, she weaves you in and out of her life. Transformed, you step to the same sinuous rhythms with the she-cat. You glide along eons of dusty hallways and bookshelves, not wanting to stop until you are in the luxurious surroundings that only two cats could truly appreciate. The walls are large stones, the hearth enormous with a fire roaring in front of an alpaca rug. Soft cushions are everywhere, velvet no doubt. You pad around the room together, inspecting the furniture with your paws and noses. Suddenly, the perfect pillow materializes on the rug in front of the fire. A cut-glass bowl appears next to the cushion, as you realize your companion, the Korat, is already seated in a French Provincial settee to your right. Next to her, a petit table with an identical crystal bowl, is gleaming in the rainbow colors of the fire. The bowl fizzles . . . champagne, but of course! For two cats on the red carpet to the stars, we are nowhere and everywhere. Champagne Sisters, unite!

Linda (Leen-da)

That's Luscious, to you, hon. Wanton and watery, she looks up at you from the depths, rippling under the surface. You only see a little of her at first. Your eyes become accustomed to the water, are you underwater or on top? She slips you under the surface with her and the world is suddenly bright, iridescent and sparkling as you thought only the world of stars could be. Fishes big and small, blue ones, yellow ones, striped ones of every variety melt past you, darting in and out of the jungle-like kelp rising statuesquely from the sea floor. Swimming becomes easier, the large, sleek fin extending from your waist propelling you alongside her, behind her, in front of her; she allowing you whatever position of flight you require at the time. Together you swim with the dolphins, whales, manta rays—flinging themselves out of the water with the lack of resistance that is felt only in deep space. That's the question with this Lady of the Watery Stars: Are you under the stars, with the fish, out amongst the stars looking back or, for that matter, does anyone care?

Marylin

With placid expression and relaxed mouth, she floats in and out of the world as she used to see it. Tall, youngster mountains look down upon her reassuringly. She feels the touch of their Love, and it settles her into the seat of the little truck just that much more. Like a well-worn book, flung open at a favorite passage, she takes in everything around her with no need for words. The words are already written; she will commit them to paper later.

Now is for inhaling the exquisite perfume of the verdant mountainsides, acres of *cevala*[25] and her favorite, the musty, woolen odor of the people of the mountains. Unable to bottle it, she prefers the soft, magical aroma of their weavings instead. Being transported to a favorite memory is easy this way; one whiff of the small, colorful *mesa*[26] and she is instantly back inside a dark, smoky kitchen. With women and little children on the floor, they are preparing dinner while a small fire burns quietly in the corner. The baby never lacks for

25   cevala: a wheat-like grain, used for making beer.
26   mesa: a Peruvian ceremonial weaving, used as a table on the ground.

love or attention; a mother, a father, or a favorite aunt will always see to the child's needs. Unobtrusive talk goes on around her. She catches some of the Spanish, but there is no need for literal understanding because the language of Love and cosmic energy is universal. A new calmness washes over her like a gentle waterfall. Is she underwater? At one with all that surrounds her, no need to communicate, she closes her eyes and she slips under the surface, never losing the smell of the roasting lamb in the clay oven next to her.

Tom

Tom of the shifting eyes, the hard eyes, the eyes of crystal that see out into the stars where we all will go eventually. The creases, time-worn into his face, are creases of many a day gone by, probably a few million years' worth. But notice the location of the creases; the mouth that is quick to show the gap between the teeth with an uproarious laugh. The eyes that will dance a little jig right when he has you all cozy and comfortable and about to come in for the kill. The Kill of Love, that is.

The Love of this Universe lays him open to predators and friends alike; it is a chance he takes because he loves so fiercely. He is here on this planet to make sure those of us who are intent upon returning to the stars, with all the others intact, won't get away this time. Like a magnet you are pulled, becoming a magnet yourself and pulling in the others, as you all move along the dusty, sensuous, nose-caking road of twinkling, spiritual delight.

TWO

Cycles
of Life

My Mother, My Teacher, My Friend

Querido Waiki,

So far, the stories and letters have been written with you in mind as the primary reader. But living a life guided by Love and intent has so changed me, that it has affected all of my relationships—family, friends and passing acquaintances. So now, as the writing progresses, let me periodically share with you letters and stories written to other loved ones in my life, that you may fully appreciate my Love of connection, kinship and all the cycles of life, death and rebirth. My Mother, My Teacher, My Friend illustrates just a sliver of the incredible relationship between my mother and me.

The words echo in my mind:

"I don't hear whiny voices."

"This is for your own good."

"Someday you'll look back on this and understand."

"Do you want to make some cookies together?"

"Come on now, let me see you sparkle . . . c'mon, sparkle! There you go!"

"You can do anything you set your mind to!"

"You just go to your room until you've got a better attitude!"

"I'm so proud of you!"

Who said these words? I did.

Who else said these words? You did.

By example and with love that was sometimes tough, you gave me a foundation to be a wonderful mother.

In desperation, I reached out for advice when my own little one was difficult.

"What do I do when Morgan won't let me feed him?"
"He's trying to tell you he can do it himself; give him things he can
    hold."
"Yogurt isn't my idea of finger food!"

Then there was adolescence.
God, I must have been a difficult teenager!
I never said I was sorry.
My dearest Mother, I regret the pain of concern I caused you.
By loving me through all my difficulties you taught me how to raise a
    beautiful teenager.
He doesn't give me near the grief I must have given you. Thank you.

So many memories wash over me on this lovely day to honor you and
    to be honored:
Five years old, blue sky, yellow hills, all my siblings at school and I
    have Mother all to myself.
Back deck, bright sun, little pool, I laugh with my naked, happy boy
    with curls.
Roses in the garden, forsythia in yellow bloom, Mother is proud as I
    stand in Communion white.
I stand proudly, listening as my son tells me how he helped his friend
    at camp "with that energy thing" because she was homesick and
    missed her family.

We are different, yet so much alike.
You gave me a lot of love to pass on, as you continue to every day.
Thank you, I love you.

Mother's Day, May 1998

Amalia's Fairy Tale

Dear Waiki,

This was a gift I wrote for my aunt on her birthday. You remember my tía Amalia[27] from Málaga; she and my Uncle Erwin came to our camp up in Williams for a day. Both she and Uncle Erwin wished they could have spent more time with us. She came curious, and walked away with a more diverse understanding of Love.

From far away she came to join our family. She didn't sound like us or look like us. She looked like a fairy princess. Thick, blonde plaits of hair, royal blood I'm sure, high cheekbones and a definite regal air to her walk. Beautiful children followed in her wake. She acclimated, she went to the seashore for surfing and burgers and she almost fit in. But she still didn't talk like the other moms and she still looked like royalty. There was an attitude to the tilt of her head, a take charge approach to life that suggested no compromise.

Until you looked in her eyes. That is what gave her away and still does today. In her eyes you see the agelessness of her soul, the laughter and joy of being a mother, the fierceness with which she protects her young, even to this day. The laughter, yes, the laughter is in her eyes and on her lips! She lives life intensely for her children, her husband, then herself. Her dear friends mean more to her than her own safekeeping. Surely they would tell you she would do all for any of them. And still, she looks like the queen of everything.

When I say she almost fit in, this is indeed a compliment. Because to have Amalia assimilate completely into the American culture would have been a heartbreak. With her persistent Spanish accent, the head-up royal walk, we can all be assured that fairy tales still exist. We thank you, Amalia, for reminding us to always shoot for the stars.

27 Amalia: Amalia Rice of Málaga, Spain. She married my uncle, Erwin Rice in 1948, and subsequently had five children. As cousins we were all very close, especially after they moved to Prescott from Palos Verdes, California, in 1965. My father and Uncle Erwin worked together for many years.

Afternoon With Erwin

Dear Uncle Erwin,

I had a beautiful vision today while working with you.[28] A golden eagle came flying by, wings full spread, circling you as you lay sleeping. It circled and dipped, circled and dipped, coming to rest finally and ever so gently on your bed. Proudly and with assurance, it walked around you on the soft down comforter, coming to rest above you on the pillow to your right, watching you silently, encouraging you to rest.

I wondered as I watched: Of what significance was this? What did this beautiful bird represent? As I continued to observe, the eagle settled down, using your pillow as it would a nest, settling into sleep. As I watched the raptor, it was transformed to a downy white dove. There was brilliant light and a soft, quiet feeling to the room. Then I realized I was watching your own Spirit assist you in your sleep. It continued to transform for whatever comfort you might need, llama hides for warmth, cooling Andean snow for the heat, soft white bunnies surrounding you, keeping you quiet and warm. All you have to do is ask, and it is all there waiting for you.

You have a gift of genuine kindness and openness to all people; this is why you are so receptive to this work. It is your openness and receptiveness returning to help you at this time. It is an honor to assist you in this work of Love.

---

28   Erwin Rice: see note, Amalia's Fairy Tale. My uncle had cancer, and was unable to sleep. He slept solidly for the first time in two weeks after the we did shamanic healing work together.

For Father's Day

What can I possibly give you on Father's Day? A hug, a card, a poem, a kiss? None of these say what's truly in my heart. How can they? Someone else's idea on a card that speaks of my love for you? My experiences with you? Our many heart-to-heart talks, sometimes in the still of the dark night?

No, nobody's words but my own can tell you of the many eyes of the storm we've gone through together. Tossed around by love and misunderstanding, sometimes so close as to see the flecks of color in the other's iris, sometimes so far away we didn't know the other existed. Caught up in the storm of each other's love, each of us has alternately pushed and pulled at the other, thinking he or she had something we needed, only to find it hidden in ourselves. Only to find our Love for each other grown stronger when we weren't looking.

How did it all happen? The past is past, no need to wonder; the present is now, where our love grows daily. What does the future hold? That's up to us. It seems the best thing to do is what we're doing right now, holding on to each other with Love in the calm of the eye of the storm, with only one intent: to Love one another as we are, no exceptions, completely, as two people raising each other up, as we move through this thing we call life.

You have passed on much and I am grateful. You held on to me during the storms, even though I wasn't aware of it. You helped bring me up and continue to show me boundless kindness and love. You should know how much of your kindness and generosity are passed on to others through me. You taught me well.

Thank you, I love you.
Happy Father's Day,
Your Baby

Onions and Love

My Dearest Waiki,

Not all is beauty and bliss. There is death, loss, birth and rebirth. Does everyone feel this way? Tossed around by the ravages of life, looking out serenely from my rose-colored glasses, it is inevitable, I feel. So many changes, so fast, where to begin?

The world is moving so quickly, there are babies having babies. That is how it seems. And now my baby is a young man. No longer a baby at all, and the mother must let go. Letting go . . . . There is so much to let go of, but my culture tells me, "Hold On! Guide him with your wisdom, tell him to drive safely, to practice safe sex." But it is too late for that. I've already said it. And either he heard it or he didn't. Now I must step back and look at my handiwork. Did I do enough? Love enough? Yes, I know I did, yet that inevitable paranoia of motherhood creeps in and I want to shout, "Be careful! Don't!" Don't what? If I keep saying "don't," he will. I would. Either he heard it or he didn't.

And, still, there are onions to peel. Bushels and bushels of onions. Cultural onions. Layers upon layers of eye-smarting, nose-watering, breath-catching onions. And not just one, as many think. I am committed to exploring how many onions in this lifetime I can peel, so my son and his sons and daughters after him have fewer onions to peel. Looking upon the culture, what is worth keeping and what do we toss away? Embedded deep in our unconscious, our culture tells us how to react, respond, talk, think, behave, love, whom to love and how. What's the best way. The best way? Something as indefinable as Love; can someone else tell me what is the best way to love?

This is my experience of Universal Love: diving into a slippery pool of Jell-O-like substance, ancient beings bumping against my formless soul. Moving from this three-dimensional reality to the other side where there is stillness, a silence that goes beyond any concept of what our ears know. Feeling a warm, inviting presence between my hands expand as big as the planet, all the while engulfing me, entering me with a sensation I have learned to know as Love.

It is the ability to converse with the Cosmos, to feel that distinct, different dimension, to know diverse realities, that makes it a bit easier to be human, to be a mother, and to let go. We are always One, there is no separation.

There Is No Time

Recently, while reading an article on the *Q'ero* prophecies, I was reminded of an experience I had three years ago. This particular article was discussing a possible warp in the time continuum. In this future time of *pacha kuti*,[29] the great change, one could move in and out of different time and reality spaces. I'm never quite sure what to think of any prophecy, even from my beloved *Q'ero*. It seems that as each moment moves past us, the possibility of a future happening occurring as predicted can change. Maybe the prophecy is already true, as I know people now who can move about in many different planes and spaces.

While sitting in my hot tub one contemplative, star-filled evening, I asked the *Q'ero* waikis to share with me an experience. I am in the habit of conversing telepathically with my waiki friends on a regular basis; for me it is like picking up the telephone. I discussed this with Américo on my first trip to Perú.

With trepidation, speaking to him in Spanish, I told him that whenever I spoke to him, when I was in Arizona and he was in Perú, I always heard him in English. As we never conversed on the telephone, he immediately took my meaning. His delighted response, given with a slight smile was, "And when you speak to me . . . it is always in Spanish." I knew then I wasn't imagining things, and thereafter completely accepted this form of communication.

Now, back to the experience and the evening in question. As I sat staring at the large juniper tree in the backyard, I was struck with my profound ability to focus on the particular moment. The tree, as the object of my awareness and single focus, was the only thing that existed. Speaking remarkably slowly, I voiced, "Wow! So this is why you do this . . . it's like time has completely stopped." In my ears I heard a rumbling laugh and delighted voices say "Time? What time?"

---

29   pacha kuti: A stepping outside of time. See glossary.

All of my surroundings, the rest of the yard, the spa and the buildings, slowly returned for my consideration. There was a slow motion and surreal quality to it all. The meaty, mysterious laughter continued and slowly faded away as I returned to this present reality.

I am reminded that Time is a man-made construct that we can leave behind anytime we wish. And one I would certainly encourage.

Morgan Drives

Dearest Waiki,

The blank page stares out at me waiting for the newest encounter, the newest experience to convey to you. There are many right now; it is difficult to sort through and decide which to write about in the here and now. Some chronology is probably helpful, so I'll begin at the beginning.

An important chapter in my life has closed and a new one has opened. It feels more like a book, really. Children do grow up and move away from you, either symbolically or literally, and the challenge is in seeing the beauty and appropriateness of the sequence. Let me just write about my feelings right now. I think that will speak more eloquently of my state of being.

The vision was fulfilled. On a hot July day the confident young man grabbed his soccer gear of cleats, shorts and bag and headed out of the house. Tossing his bag in the Jeep as if he'd done it a thousand times, he climbs in. The moment is surreal. I beg off a telephone call to watch. Closing the door, he claims his new mount. Just a millisecond of eternity passes as we watch each other and know something very different is about to enter our lives. In our bizarre culture of TV, loud music, fast cars and speeding airplanes, this is the rite of passage for our young people. More so for the young men, so they can leave their mothers behind in the ultimate cutting-of-the-apron-strings ceremony. The engine roars in my ears; can it possibly be that loud? With a bit of a grind as the car is placed in reverse, my heart begins its own lurch.

I knew this day was coming, I saw this for the last six months, I'm prepared, right? Are we ever, truly? The car creeps backward toward the street. Have I said everything I was supposed to? Smoothly he maneuvers the car into first gear and begins the descent down our little street. Again our eyes meet, he waves, he is gone. As I watch from the porch, the car drives away from me, down the street, just as I envisioned. Odd about that, literally as I saw it for those many months, and now the moment is passed. No matter how many times we prepare ourselves, moments like this have an unknown quality. I saw what was to happen so as to prepare myself for what to feel, not realizing I could never prepare myself fully for the gaping hole I felt in my heart, the one that seemed to whistle with my breath.

In a daze I return to the house, heading for my favorite chair that awaits me, welcoming me with its large, overstuffed softness. Like a movie screen before me, reels of moving pictures from the past fly by my consciousness. Morgan is only 13 months old in this rerun, and the rain is coming down in the big droplets characteristic of the summer rain storm just about to unleash buckets of water. Curiously he ventures out into the rain, crouching a bit as the spheres of water drop all around him and plop, plop down on his little head and shoulders. With the wonder only a child can exhibit, he looks skyward attempting to discover the source of the water. The rain increases, he squeals with delight and dashes on unsteady legs back under the shelter, toward safety, toward Mom. He clutches tightly for just a moment, then runs back out to explore his new found world of rain.

The deluge begins in earnest now. He is laughing, loving it, my heart is full to bursting as he, too, enjoys my favorite season of the year. From the sanctity of the shelter we stand silently, fulfilled, watching the downpour. It is no wonder this particular memory came back to me now. I still see that sense of wonder in him in experiencing new things, and I still stand waiting, ready to be told of the delight of the world.

Renewal at the Farm

Dear Waiki,

There is a special sanctuary near my home. Cynthia Gardner and Hank Schrieber have made me welcome there for many years, and I am honored to be considered family. You know how important family is to me. Summer is especially sweet, when the land is parched, the water cool and the friendships abundant.

Ahh, the land, la tierra. Stark and yellow, the hot wind blows the last ounce of moisture out of the bent blade of grass. The bull stands as a lone sentinel guarding the water as it rushes through the concrete stream bed on its way to water something, somewhere else. Strange, this bull. Cartoon-like, never moving, not even an ear. Large doe-eyes, the face strangely out of sync with the large gray hump on his back. He is beautiful, dove gray in color, enormous in size and presence. But is he real? Still, he does not move as I pass over the rickety bridge that appears ready to fall into the water below. With dust following my truck like a magnet, I slowly move on.

Joyful to be in the open spaces, birds everywhere dive and flit past the vehicle as it maneuvers down the road. Weeds just inches high, scorched by the elements of Nature. Where do all these birds come from? Hundreds are flushed out as I reach my destination.

Brown adobe walls, junk yard filled beyond capacity, yet tucked neatly behind its tall, weathered fence. The Farm welcomes me home, ready to strip me bare and cleanse my very soul. It's really not a farm in the classic sense. But truly many things grow here. Little children challenge the bigger ones, all learning in the process. Love especially grows here, waiting for me in myriad forms of frigid water, hot sun and unrelenting wind with the cool, dark office always available to envelop me with its secrets of magic and commerce.

Cynthia's Tower stands as a lighthouse guiding family and friends to this lush sanctuary. It is my favorite. Two stories high, it rises skyward as if awaiting Rapunzel to let down her hair. In the lower level, the shadowy room offers a pleasurable chill contrasted by the warmth of the energy which is Cynthia. Everywhere there are books of many a different taste and caliber. Classics sit stoically among the tomes to Goddesses and Magic. Spear Finger, the granite goddess of the tower, watches over me as I survey the room with fondness, bent on a relaxing siesta. The large, built-in window seat beckons with pillows for my luxurious nap. Knowingly, I pull one from the multicolored heap and fling it to the middle of the I-don't-know-what-kind-of-furry, large, soft rug that is my sleeping preference. The hours disappear into the early-evening sweetness of sunset, wine and family, in the shade of an adobe wall.

After discovering all the answers to the universe, sleepily I move to bed. The evening is young yet and there are wall-to-wall stars. I climb the sturdy, wooden staircase to the upper level of the Tower, happily drinking in the Milky Way. My thirst quenched, I bed down in Cynthia's upper room of artful, Little People, surrounded by windows with twinkling jewels shining through. Drifting to dreamland now, in what once was the Tower, and is now the top of my rocket ship to the heavens.

Love Glows

The light dances off the towering trees above me, the water droplets hanging on the branches awaiting the fairies for their removal. This place, this little bit of heaven called Waianapanapa in Hana, Maui, beckons to me to relax, release the self, delve into the solid, volcanic world of the *menehune*.[30] The surf pounds the rocks below; she rakes the stones with her fingers, then heads back out to sea. There are many people here, tourists mostly, walking with the purpose of seeing all of the rain forest in one day. There are others, walking more slowly, taking in the novelty of the plumeria-scented jungle mixed with the sharp tang of the salt air. Other drifters look to find their way home. Some seem to have come home already; some will not find their home in this lifetime, too fearful to make the plunge of Faith it takes to ensure their next step.

The people who share this expedition with me are a group of individuals hoping to better their spirits and lives, traveling on an inward journey with the assistance of an Andean mystic. Our adventure for the day is another magical journey on this mystical isle of Maui, a place of intrigue known only to me as "Big Mama." Feminine names abound here. A friend once said, "To take a woman to Hawaii is like taking sand to the beach." All my body knows is that the slower rhythm of my walk feels much more natural and satisfying than the hurried pace of "The Mainland."

Into this realm Al walks. Cautious and respectful of the land, the people, the signs and the energy, quietly he approaches when our circle breaks up. My friends welcome him like a warm cottage welcomes its master upon his return. He is welcomed as a dear friend, too long since last parting. Small talk is made, plans for the day are arranged; Al will join the group and enjoy our excursions to the many places others go, but few realize.

30   menehune: fairy-like creatures in the Hawaiian tradition.

Into this circle of Love and friendship I strolled. I'm pleased to see the man who assisted us with the trivialities and necessities of everyday life just a few days ago. It was a few days past that now seem a very distant memory. The memories have been altered by the magic of the rain forest, the mist, the warm sun, the crashing waves and conversations on the value of Universal Love.

My only intent is to say thanks for his gift of assistance on the other side of the island. To say, "Hello, nice to see you again," before I turn once again to the land that has captured my heart, and then return to listen to the voice of the Mother, by myself, just as I have been for years. My body moving to a different rhythm, slowly I reach over for a friendly hug to give my appreciation to this nice man. Something shifts. Through me moves the most sensuous, beaming rocket of pulsing light that is conceivable. I become aware that I have just given the most meaningful embrace of my life. Stuttering, the words difficult to slide out of my mouth, comes a puzzled, inquiring "Hi there . . . " as I look into the face of a stranger that is literally glowing back at me with a confused but delighted look upon his face. The moment stretches into eternity, still we hold each other in this tender caress. Staring at the radiance that is bouncing off our faces, he responds with a surprised "Well, . . . hello!" as we continue our vibrant, energetic introduction. No thought enters my mind. I swim in this oscillating, fiery conflagration that has me rooted to this bit of insignificant grass, looking into the soul of someone I've not seen in 1000 years. It has been *such* a long time. Slowly we come back to real time, still staring at each other in awe, joyful for our rediscovery and not able to take our eyes or our bodies away from the miracle of each other. Giddy and shy, we hesitate a bit before releasing the other, not wanting the enchantment to cease, still unsure of what we just witnessed. We then become aware we are not alone, in fact, our two dear friends have just observed this dynamic dialogue. With smiles of knowing on their faces, all they can utter is a surprised "Wow!" The group is forming behind us, oblivious to the exchange or transformation, ready to go on another quest. I turn as I've done in other lives and reach back to take his hand. There is a split second of surprise, then in agreement, he grasps mine as we walk toward the sea.

The two of us take our place at the back of the line, traversing the sharp volcanic rock with ease, lost in idle conversation, fulfilling dreams lost long ago to both of us, reborn of a moment's enlightenment. Our conversation sounds to others as two people beginning a friendship; to us it is a coming home, a passionate drama already rehearsed, the lines memorized, each one waiting for a partner to play.

The day progresses as we move in and out of each other's reality, both being careful, not overeager, testing the waters. Night falls and the others are asleep. Talking long and late, it's now two in the morning and we need sleep. Neither of us wanting to leave this delicious bubble, not wanting to share our bodies; this is too important. An agreement is made for full clothing, above-the-covers-snuggling, and we fall into an easy sleep in each other's arms. Having not slept with another for years, I'm amazed in the morning that I slept so well.

Al leaves in the morning for the other side of the island and work. In sorrow and excitement we part, aware there is something very electrifying about the connection we share. At the end of the day I can't contain myself and call him on the phone. Sleepily he answers and reveals he was just thinking about me and we discuss the synchronicity of my phone call. He is coming back to Hana tomorrow. His boss took one look at him and said upon his request for time off, "Whoever she is, take three days, not two." I'm dancing on air; could this really be "It?"

The following day finds me staying close to home. Al is to arrive at six. I hound my roommate Linda to get us to the house by five. The news is spreading; who is this man? The story of our magical meeting is received with warmth and love. I realize there is no course but one. Does he feel this way? In excitement I prepare myself in a flowery gown, awaiting his arrival. Another has taken over my kitchen duties for me to fuss, I'm like a girl on her first date.

I hear the truck before anyone else, and I'm out the door and headed for the stairs in a flash, aware that my two friends, Linda and Leah, are watching the scene from above. I don't care. As I descend the stairs, with my back to the driveway, I realize Al has not gotten out of his truck, and with delicious, romantic awareness I know he is riveted watching me float down the stairs. As I turn the corner he is staring, and has not moved from his place behind the wheel. Now time truly moves in slow motion. He exits the truck, our eyes never moving from each other's. Suddenly, we are now inches apart, and stop and stare, captured by the glow that emanates from both of us. The glow, the radiance that continues to this day to capture our hearts, our bodies and our souls, this beautiful golden light is everywhere, in and around us. Swiftly we find ourselves in each others' arms, kissing, hugging, laughing, smiling, and yes, glowing.

We hurry through our dinner tasks, eventually finding ourselves alone on the back lanai, the moment of truth at hand. Al utters something passionate to the effect of wanting me completely. Body and soul, he wants it all. Looking him dead in the eye I reply, "You'll have to wait." I have dreamt of this moment, to find the right man who was worth waiting for, who knew I was worth waiting for in the sanctity of marriage. He quickly grasps the old-fashioned concept of marriage and sexual union and with amazement at himself replies, "I know!"

"So what are we waiting for? Is this real or not? Are you going to get down on your knees or what?" I hear myself saying. Instantly, he slides to his knee and says "Like this?" We draw closer, foreheads touching, hearts wrapped around each others' lives. "So, will you marry me?" "Yes, definitely yes, I will," came my immediate reply.

Alfred John Petrich stayed on his knees for 45 minutes asking Marilyn Ann Markham to marry him, long after she had assured him she would, 48 hours after they had seen each other for the first time. They were married two weeks later on her birthday in Maui, Hawaii, unable to wait any longer to be the husband and wife they already knew they were. They live a life of glowing, glorious love, sharing this story every opportunity they have.

Wedding Day

The last time I looked, the clock read 12:30 a.m. I drifted off for another hour before the clock provided its rude awakening. The purpose of the awakening wasn't rude; just the hour and the irritating buzzer going off in my ear. It was my wedding day! I was excited and nervous about our upcoming adventure, but not at all nervous about the ceremony we would share later in the afternoon.

Let me begin at the beginning. My betrothed, Al, was a tour guide on The Mountain in Maui, Hawaii. It was known otherwise as Haleakala, the dormant volcano, and he worked for *Maui Mountain Cruisers*. Visitors are taken by van, in the early hours of the morning, up the steep, twisting, 38 miles to the summit, at 10,023 feet. The guides' job is to give visitors historical facts about the area, crack corny jokes, or anything else that will keep them awake at three in the morning. After watching the predawn colors blend into sunrise, the tourists mount bicycles and cruise down the mountain, an exhilarating ride full of beautiful views, fog, a little rain and breakfast near the bottom. Those people who were unsure of their ability on a bike, could ride down in the van, now being able to appreciate the scenery that was dark a few hours earlier.

I'd never done the bike ride before, but this had been Al's job and passion for the last six years. He took great pride in his work, teaching the clients about Maui and her volcano, all the while keeping a close eye on them, keeping them safe. He had made nearly a thousand trips down the mountain and referred to it as "my office."

So, we got up with the alarm, and I felt fuzzy after such little sleep. But the shower woke me up and we were down to the baseyard by 2:00. We took a van to Lahaina, on the west side of the island, to pick up sleepy clients from their hotels.

Later, for the drive up the mountain, Al would have a driver, as he is the cruise leader on these trips. That means he is the lead bike rider coming down the mountain, twisting and turning on his seat to look behind him. He checks on his group to make sure everything is going smoothly, with nobody getting too close to another rider, while the driver brings up the rear, protecting the group and letting Al know when there is traffic that needs to get by.

On this first leg of the journey, however, he was picking up passengers by himself. He was getting to know them, and sizing them up to make sure no one was intoxicated, had any health problems they hadn't told him about, or anything else that could cause an issue with safety at the top of the mountain or on the ride down.

Visitors to Maui are often fooled about the trip up to the top of Haleakala, feeling they're on a tropical island, so what's the big deal? The big deal is that you are driving from sea level to 10,000 feet—two miles up—and 10,000 feet is 10,000 feet no matter where you are. It's windy and cold up there, and a lot of landlubbers have difficulty breathing at that altitude. Many people haven't been on a bicycle in years, and to ride a bike on such a scenic highway, sharing it with cars and buses, not to mention all the curves, makes for a bit more danger than the ticketing agents lead them to believe. *Maui Mountain Cruisers* is one of the companies that does take it all seriously, making sure its clients have a fun, memorable experience at the same time.

After we collected the clients from the hotels, we returned to the baseyard. They were given coffee and pastries to help them wake up, while Al and his driver hooked up the bike trailer and prepared to go. I kept to myself, chatting a bit with some of the tourists, but mostly I'm not a morning person and this definitely qualified as morning! Al had not mentioned to his clients who I was in relationship to him, so taking his cue, I didn't enlighten any of them.

Once we were all loaded in the van, Al made sure I sat in the seat directly behind the front passenger seat. I was looking forward to a little snooze or staring out the window in the dark. How wrong I was! Al jumped in the van while I wondered how anybody could be so vibrant at that hour. He turned around in the front seat and strapped himself in. When he began his introduction I realized he intended to do the whole drive that way; as "in my face" as anyone could possibly get. This is the side of him I'd not yet seen, the extrovert, the comedian, the completely in charge-funny-dude who takes his job very seriously. But the trip up was fun, and a few people stayed awake to talk about the islands with Al.

After we got all the clients sorted out, we showed them where to stand for the sunrise for the best view. Then the two of us hiked to the top of White Hill, where we had our own private wedding ceremony planned. We had wanted to have a formal wedding up at the top, but it is a National Park and that would have required all sorts of red tape. So we opted for an unofficial wedding of hearts.

There I was, in all of my wedding finery: a large, blue rainsuit over other layered, cold weather gear. I felt like the Pillsbury Dough Boy. Al was in his wedding duds, too: a large, brown, down jacket, faded from the Hawaiian sun, with an odd, diagonal dark line that runs from shoulder to hip, from the radio he wears while riding. Over-sized black jeans finished the outfit, with ample room for long underwear and bike shorts underneath, along with a jaunty red handkerchief tied around his neck for warmth.

At the rising of the sun, my romantic love blew his bamboo flute, sounding like a conch shell, to symbolize the beginning of our life together. He presented me with a ring, and asked me to be his wife, all the while telling me how I had brought such joy to his life. He told me he would never leave my side and we were partners for this life and other lives to come. I was speechless and overwhelmed by his tender words, my words came haltingly and choked by tears. I simply nodded and asked him to be my husband always, of my heart, by my heart. "Will you be mine?" "Yes, yes," each of us responded to the other, and we held each other and kissed. A couple nearby was happy to take our picture and we left our mountaintop to check on Al's clients.

After gathering at the van, Al told the group our exciting news. Promptly, a small bottle of champagne was produced from some-where at the back of the van. After congratulations were given all around, I settled down for a short nap before we left the mountain. I have always appreciated my ability to catnap when necessary, and never as much as on that day. Al had been very specific about safety and making sure we were up for the ride. I knew I was groggy from lack of sleep, and wasn't going to ride the bicycle unless I felt wide awake and invigorated.

I snapped awake twenty minutes later, as energy surged through me and I knew I could make the ride safely. Before I knew it, we were all headed down the mountain, with me right behind Al, enjoying every breathtaking moment. At each turn was a new view of either eucalyptus forest, the island of Maui, or blue-green ocean, spreading off in the distance. We pulled over periodically to take goofy snapshots, or just to check the group and let a tour bus go by. We stopped for a leisurely breakfast in Kula, stripped off the big coats and made our way down the hill. The day had just begun.

We left the baseyard by 11:00 in a bit of a hurry, as we had a one o'clock appointment scheduled with the Justice of the Peace in Wailuku. This is where all the official, legal things happen on the island. We sped for home to shower and get into our real wedding clothes and prepared for the ceremony that would bind us by all the laws of the land.

Al left me to my own preparations while he went to pick up our leis. The moment he walked in the door I knew for sure I had made the right decision to marry him. In walked my transplanted Texan; dressed in a black and white Hawaiian shirt with just the perfect hang to it, tucked into snug fitting, black jeans and boots. The smile on his face and the excited banter he shared with his best man spoke volumes to me. He literally took my breath away. It wasn't just the look or his behavior, it's that indefinable something, the energy of the man that told me we were matched for each other.

Before I knew it there we were, standing solemnly in front of the judge in his office, ready to proceed. When I noticed his book shaking a bit, I chuckled to myself at the irony. I was standing rock solid and the judge was nervous! He began to address us with the usual words "We are gathered together today, to witness this union . . . ." For five seconds I stood at attention and looked properly at the official in front of us. Then, realizing this was not what I wanted to do, I took a deep, pleasant breath, swiveled my head to the right and stared into my loved one's eyes for the rest of the ceremony.

The judge uttered the words, "and now I pronounce you husband and wife." There was a long silence while he contemplated something, looking at his toes. "Kiss the bride?" Al inquired. "No, I'm not done!" the judge stated firmly. Gathering his thoughts, he continued. "You will have many obstacles to face together. There will be many who oppose you. You must be steadfast and keep your own counsel." "My Lord," I thought! He wasn't kidding! How did he know we were walking into a hornet's nest the minute we landed on the mainland? I had gone away to work with a spiritual group in Maui for two weeks and I would return, three weeks later, a married woman! You bet there was going to be opposition! He continued with other beautiful words of encouragement and finally did let Al kiss his bride.

Waiki, I wanted to share with you the beauty of our day, knowing you and Velquis[31] were there in Spirit. Later in the afternoon, Tom, Bobbi and Linda celebrated in Prescott with us. We drank champagne together, while laughing and rejoicing over the phone. It couldn't have been a more beautiful day. There is simply nothing more to add.

31   Velquis Yábar: Américo's wife.

Al's Homecoming

Mi Querido Waiki,

Laughing with another mother the other day about young people's antics, I knew you would get a good chuckle out of Al's first encounter with my son, Morgan. Without any rites of passage or acknowledgment of transition from young person to adult, it can be difficult to be a teenager in the Western culture. They often flounder trying to prove their ability in the adult world; they often choose alcohol as their means of proof.

To say Morgan was angry with me for going to Hawaii to work with you and a spiritual group, and then coming home with a husband, is an understatement. He was not only livid, he was hurt that he had no say in the matter of our marriage and had to meet Al after the fact. I did indeed feel for him and thought he had every right to feel the way he did. At the age of 16 he had become the "man of the house," not a rightful position but one that often happens in single parent homes. He was taller and stronger than I now, and delighted in being able to help in those capacities. For the most part, he hadn't shared me with anyone else for ten years; we were close and I knew trouble loomed in the distance. It would be all right in the end and it was, but we had to get over this first hurdle. Al and I knew there was a lot riding on his and Morgan's first meeting.

Arriving late from Hawaii via Phoenix, Al and I were looking forward to a cold beer in the cantina and a long sleep. I looked forward to showing off my son and my home to my husband and vice-versa. As we got out of the car and stretched, Morgan and his friend Patrick came outside to greet us.

"Mom! I'm so glad to see you, I *really* missed you!" With a goofy smile on his face, Morgan moved toward me with much enthusiasm and gave me a hug, throwing his arm over my shoulder. My head reeled back from the impact of the liquor on his breath.

"So, been drinking a little, Morgan?" I assessed the situation and the steadiness of his stance.

"Just a little . . . " he replied, still with that silly look on his face and a slight weave in his walk. I was glad he had chosen to be truthful.

Introductions were made and Morgan and Al silently and politely looked each other over. I observed both boys carefully as we headed into the house.

When I left for Hawaii a full-scale remodel of my kitchen was underway. Now everything from my kitchen was in my living room fighting for space. A friend had agreed to check on Morgan periodically; he had wanted the responsibility of being on his own. I wasn't expecting an immaculate house under those conditions, but what assailed my senses when I stepped in the door was difficult to comprehend. A fine, thick grit covered every surface in the house. Dirty dishes covered the few available surfaces. There were piles of sheets and towels in various stages of cleanliness on the couch, the chair and the floor, while the linen closet stood open as if an explosion had occurred inside. Speechless, I wandered around as Morgan made halting explanations for what lay in front of me.

"I'm sorry, Mom . . . I got real mad after you called and I guess I kind of lost it." Looking like a lost lamb, he continued. "We had a party . . . oh! the towels? Well, the toilet got plugged up and over-flowed—so we mopped it up with those. Donna came over the next day and helped me clean up—she told me to put everything away—but I just didn't get it all done." I wondered at that point what *had* gotten done.

"What about the toilet, now?" I inquired as I lifted the lid. I wished I hadn't. Morgan was beginning to look green as he continued his now incredibly feeble excuse. "Some girl came up to use the toilet, not knowing there was a problem. I guess she had to . . . well . . . ." Yes, I could see what she had had to do in the toilet.

There was no reason to continue this discussion. I sent the boys to bed with the promise to wake them up early, in time for their double shift at the restaurant where they both worked. It was Labor Day weekend; at least I drew pleasure from the fact they would be working very long, hard hours with hangovers.

I turned to my husband of 36 hours and said with little enthusiasm and much embarrassment, "Welcome home!" Al had been quiet, not saying anything, letting me handle Morgan and the situation, wandering around his new home. Al is nothing short of a class act, and the first words out of his mouth as he rolled up his sleeves in the bathroom were, "You got a snake for the toilet?" After turning my eyes toward heaven with an acknowledgment of extreme gratitude, I happily ventured toward the basement to show him where all the tools were kept. Much later, we had that cold beer.

Fairies and Tigers

Dearest Waiki,

You'll like this one, Waiki; it's filled with animals and fairies. I was in meditation when I experienced this revelation. I had broken my ribs in a small car accident, while taking Al to the airport after his first visit to Prescott, to meet my family and friends. To assist my recovery, Carla and Bruce gave me a Reiki treatment to facilitate healing.

A little history first. When I was small, living in California, I was like many children, and scared of the dark. I was sure the shadows would turn into monsters and that there were more monsters under the bed, in particular a very large tiger that, if I didn't jump off the bed, would grab my leg and pull me under. I'm not sure what I thought he would do once he got me there. I don't think I ever thought about that. Terror reigned supreme and my concern was jumping far enough off the bed to avoid the whole problem. There were, of course, repeated reassurances from my parents. The clothes were clothes, the shadows just that.

In my meditation with Bruce and Carla, I'm young again, in my bedroom in Solvang. I'm lying in my bed, looking at the shadows, afraid what they will do. I heard voices. They reassured me. "No, we aren't just shadows, we are your friends." My parents, in their love for me, told me there was nothing there. I had always known there was something there and, because I knew, I was afraid. It did not occur to me that I had an option to explore who the voices or shapes were. "No, we have always been here, we are your friends," they said. They informed me they wanted to play; they were fairies and shape-changers. "What about the people and monsters under the bed? In particular, the large-toothed tiger with the big claws?" I asked. They invited me to take a look. So, lying on my bed, I looked under the bedspread to see what was *really* under there.

First of all, everything was brown. Not black like shadows. It was all monochromatic, rather sepia. And what did I see? Cute little fairies and elves looking back at me, telling me to come play. Slowly I got down on the floor, lying flat on my belly, taking it all in. "Have you always been under here?" I inquired. "Oh, yes," they reassured me. "Won't you come play?" "But how? I won't fit!" "Yes you will, you can get down to our size if you really want to."

At that moment, I noticed my nemesis, the tiger. I started to get scared and sensing my fear, he spoke up. "Don't be afraid, I never wanted to hurt you. I just got so excited because I wanted to romp and roll on the ground with you, to play in my own rough way. I would never claw or bite you. Please, won't you come play?" Spellbound, I found myself smaller and sepia-colored. With these new dimensions, I walked under the bed. So excited he could hardly stand it, the tiger came bounding up to me, like Tigger from *Winnie the Pooh*, and the next thing I knew we were rolling and tumbling, laughing and whooping. We were having so much fun! The rest of the trolls, elves, fairies and little people watched with whoops and hollers of their own. We were all so happy to finally be together.

When we were all worn out from play, I was ready to return to the other world. I was concerned they couldn't come with me. "Of course we can! Anything that you want and believe is possible!" Hmm . . . where have I heard that before? So, we paraded out from under the bed, including the tiger of course. To my amazement we started to get bigger the minute we entered the "real" world, and turned into color! I'm thrilled to finally have my friends with me. They assure me they will always be with me and never to doubt the things I know to be true. Just remember not to go into fear first; be open to the possibilities.

As Tom Best once said, "When you open to the possibility of magic, it begins to show itself in everyday reality." How true.

Mariana Approves

Dearest Waiki,

My aunt came to see me in a dream. It was the month of September, in 1998, just three weeks after I married Al. Mariana and I had been very close while she was alive. I felt great sadness that she was not able to know Al, but Love crosses many barriers, and she evidently approves of our union. Here is the dream:

Morgan, his friend Roxey and I are at Mariana's house in Palm Springs for a vacation. We are the first ones there and are looking around. We are excited, wondering where everyone will stay, in what rooms. The house is a bit different than in real life, the terrazzo tile floor in the living room is now rough, unsealed flagstone. The wall on the south side is not there; the room simply opens up to the screened-in porch, leaving an expansive, airy feeling.

We head toward a door that is off the northwest end of the dining room and move down a hallway. We are headed for Aunt Mariana's room. The hallway has a door at the opposite end; the left wall is glass, with a door leading out to a sunny, private, little garden. I am at the far end of the hallway. We've been discussing where to put my mother and father and I suggest Mariana's room. Al enters at the opposite, far end of the hallway from me. I'm excited to see him so he can share the house tour; he hasn't been here before. Al begins moving toward me and the boys stay further down the hall, talking to each other and looking out the window. There is a strong sense of connection here, even in my dream. This home is important to me. I've had many happy times here; the house belonged to my grand-parents before it was my aunt's, and there is always family present.

Suddenly I realize we can't put Mother and Dad in Mariana's room because she will be there. I turn to Al and comment, "What am

I thinking? Mariana will be here, so . . . Well! Speak of the . . . angel!"
Mariana appears and floats down the hallway toward me. I'm so
pleased to see her, and she is beautiful in a two-piece, long, flowing
gown of midnight blue, tipped in black, crepe-de-chine. She is wearing a special necklace, a circle of gold with a narrow object, somewhat
like an arrow, that sits crossways in it. Without saying a word, she
moves past Al. She is smiling at me and takes his hand without looking back at him. Still she looks at me, floating toward me. She brings
him to me, places his hand in mine and exits through the door to her
left, into the garden, and is gone. I awaken.

Dad is Scheduled to Die

Dear Waiki,

Shortly after returning to Hawaii to spend more time with Al and celebrate our honeymoon, I had a disturbing dream about my father. It turned out to be prophetic, as well.

I awaken this morning from an enlightening dream. In the dream I am looking at my remodeled kitchen that is not quite done. The contractor breezes through, then my sister-in-law MaryAnn and my brother Fred. There seems to be a lot going on. Then suddenly, I am in a futuristic city holding a glass of wine in one hand and a napkin in the other. You know how dreams can be. My parents appear and I am aware my father is ill. My father wanders off and other people mill about. My mother moves toward me, removes the wine and napkin from my hands and sets them down on a shelf. She takes both my hands in hers. She looks me in the eye and informs me that my father is very sick, full of cancer. In order to avoid the one thing he fears the most—a long, prolonged death—they have him scheduled to die on Wednesday. In the dream it is now Friday.

Stunned, I stupidly ask, "Can you repeat that?" and the completely inconsequential "Where did it start?" Why do people ask such questions at a time like this? My mother replies, "E-Coli." "Again, please?" "E-Coli" is again the response. I realize this is not important. My mother has gone and I am left there by myself, mute. Emotions flood my body; I attempt to find my father, to talk to him, to tell him how much I love him. There he goes! I follow him, up a wide, circular staircase, calling to him, "Dad, Dad!" I realize he is drunk and unreachable. Haltingly, I stop the chase, turn and walk away. I still feel compelled to do something, yet I'm not sure what. But I do know I can be support for him on Wednesday, his day to die. Slowly I walk away, attempting to put all the pieces together.

As you can well imagine, this elicited some response in my waking life. The aspect of the dream where my father walked away feels like a metaphorical example of what he did to me the last time I was home. Symbolically, using his anger in response to my marriage, he turned his back on me. He sure picked a hell of a time to withhold love! Here I've moved halfway around the world, gotten married, going for the complete Love and Faith in the Cosmos Journey, and he decides he's gonna play little boy and pout!

As I write about this dream, I see it is important to tell him the dream, to tell him how much I love him, to ask for a connection and then not expect it. But I will tell him how I feel about him. Watching him walk away up the stairs, already drawn to something else, it appears it is time to give up the idea of a bond in my life with him. At least in the way I would like it. Just give it up.

So I called him on the telephone, all ready to tell him about my dream, to tell him how much I loved him. My mother answered and we had a nice chat. "Can I speak to Dad?" She held the phone to her body and I heard mumbled voices in the background. She returned to the phone and said, "He's watching a baseball game, honey, and really doesn't feel like talking." Boy, it sure is important not to have attachment to outcome!

My father was diagnosed with lung cancer four months later. He continues to do well after two surgeries and chemotherapy. He continues to be surprised he has survived this long and enjoys his life his way.

Dad died March 31, 2002, on Easter Sunday. It was a sad, yet joyous event. It was also a quick death, exactly as he'd hoped. Dick Markham lived life on his terms and is to be commended for that. The bond we shared the last two years of his life was the deepest and most intimate I'd ever experienced with him. We talked of many things, but of all the people he could talk to, I think he felt most comfortable with me speaking of death and what might take place on the other side due to my spiritual outlook. Although he was not a religious man, he was a good man and generous beyond belief. Speaking of his life he said, "I think I've done pretty well, I'm reasonably sure they won't roast my toes!" We've communicated since his passing, and far from having his toes warmed, he soars in the heavens. He's free and that fills me with much contentment. I love him and miss him daily.

Go for the Miracle

I am God. I am Goddess. There is no distinction or separation; I am the Collective Consciousness. I believe. I believe in the power of Love, in its healing powers, in its ability to transform the darkness to Light. I believe. I healed myself today. Healed my ribs which have been fractured, torn, contused, are generally very painful and have taken major energy from my physical body for repair.

Today I decided I wanted a complete healing. Go for the miracle, that which is not a miracle, but is seen as such because we refuse to believe that we are God and Goddess. I opened myself to all the loving energies that were available to me—Buddha, Jesus, Minerva, Apollo, Diana, Athena and Krishna—more than I can name here but I felt them all. I felt their presence, their healing power all within and around me. All my Q'ero friends, all of Américo's family, my own family and friends; I directed all that loving energy toward me first and then my ribs. I worked with my stones, deliberate movements done with infinite slowness, letting the stone do its work without my interference. I believe. I can feel the Light as it pours over my ribs, the stone doing its own work by removing the pain, the injured energy from my ribs. I know all this is possible.

I have done good work today, and there is still some work to be finished on this injury, but the pain is gone and will not return. Amen.

The Story Prince and Princess

My Waiki,

This is a gift I wrote for my aunt and uncle for their 50th wedding anniversary. You will remember them, I believe; they came to work with us in our retreat in Arizona. My uncle died a few months after this.

I have told you about the story princess from Spain and how she looked and talked so differently from the other mothers, but I never told you about her prince.

They were married after what seemed to me an incredibly romantic courtship but what do I know; I wasn't even born yet. I heard later from the two principal characters, Amalia and Erwin, that they weren't able to communicate that well due to the language difference. But hell, love never spoke louder. She, the beauty from far away; he, the incredibly nice guy with the "Aw, shucks" look on his face whenever he looked at her.

They were the original fun couple. I remember those martinis their kids talked about, those tall drinks in those frosty glasses . . . and the looks they gave each other over those glasses. Oh, how adults think children don't see things! We saw those looks and, without knowing, we understood. There always seemed to be so much going on in the Rice household at any given moment, but the story I want to tell you happened at my home, also a place of a lot of goings-on.

The fun couple has some fun relatives (my parents) who went down the Colorado River with a whole bunch of other funny people in the late 1960s. That was the time of the sexual revolution, the Beatles, long hair and letting it all hang out. Now some of you think that was for just the younger generation, but I was twelve years old and I assure you it affected some of the so-called adults, too. After the infamous running of the Colorado came the party to celebrate it all, The Slosh.

Well, as you can imagine, they all got pretty sloshed. People were done up in full costume, portraying their favorite Fugarwe Indian. This was to commemorate the last of the beer supply and something about being lost, but you'll have to ask the principal participants about the initiation. Here is what I remember about Amalia and Erwin that night.

They came dressed as I had never seen them dressed, in identical outfits. Now on Aunt Amalia, this outfit looked pretty good, she being a knockout and all, but to see Uncle Erwin in a just below-the-privates tiger skin outfit took a little getting used to! They moved in unison, drinking their drinks, taking the jokes, telling their tale of their favorite Fugarwe Indian. But then came the moment of truth. We were standing in the kitchen, Amalia and Erwin both standing in front of the sink. Some completely rude person asked my uncle to please bend over and fetch something (a sponge, perhaps, some soap?) from under the sink. Never missing a beat (and this is how I will always remember him, with complete composure and grace), he bent right down in the famous Bunny Dip, opened that cupboard and to the loud guffaws and laughter of everyone there, reached in and retrieved whatever-the-hell that person asked for and never showed more than his knees. Amalia must have shown him that. I'm not sure what else she showed him and he showed her, but they both showed me what love looks like when you find it and how to go after it and grab it for all its worth. God bless you both.

All my love,
Marilyn Markham Petrich
12-26-98

To Focus Anew

December 29, 1998

We're coming up on the last year of the century; the last few days of the year. Irony defined: Fear is what keeps me from feeling Goddess/God-like; the fear, the addiction to the indecision, then the lack of follow-through. Then putting myself down for not doing so, knowing full well I am capable of making the decision and following through to the end. So what keeps me from my Path? The fear of actually following through! Oh my God, this is so ridiculous!

So, today, I begin anew. The millennium is drawing to a close. I will attempt to write everyday about the changes occurring; in the world at large and the microscopic view I take of my own life. I hereby make the commitment to commitment, to being focused, to get off the fence, to help young people by starting with my own son, to come from Love at all times. To count to 100 when necessary, to avoid anger when I should (sometimes anger is useful), to leave the room to clean my energy when needed, to stand in Love at all times. This I commit to. I commit to my writing, to love my son, to love my husband. Oh my God, my husband! What a joy to love, nourish, enrich, enthrall and tease this lovable man. What joy I have with him, joy in the Love that emanates from us both, in finding the truest of hearts.

Christmas has just passed, and a lot of money was spent. I doubt that the joy it was to bring the world in celebration of a great man's birth was realized. Complicated times we live in. Is that cliche' or what? This changing over to a new millennium *does* feel different. First, take the possibility of global shutdown when we hit 2000, due to the inability of the computers to read 00. Such an incredibly simple thing, but it could cause the collapse of a few businesses or the frustration of the average PC owner. But potentially it also could cause global shutdowns of safety systems; hospital resources could be jeopardized; whole financial institutions could crumble; the list goes on and on.

Is this the apocalypse? It could bring an incredible new reliance on community, the whole global community. Would it be a bad thing to go back to the barter system? A barter system on a global scale? That's what my cousin does on one level, anyway. He finds one interested party who needs the recycled product belonging to another. I know there is a way to get the world's children fed; maybe it will take a grand halting of the world's consumers, including myself, to equalize things. Love the earth; love the children. Why is something so simple so difficult to accomplish? Because we have yet to accommodate the billions of people on this planet, and the exponential growth that continues and will continue if it remains unchecked. And meanwhile, more children are born into poverty and pain. This does not have to continue.

January 14, 1999

The inconsistent journaler returns. On a personal note, Al and I are moving back to Arizona from Maui, Hawaii. It has been Heaven here, even if for such a short time. Obviously, I came to Hawaii to find Al. He had asked for a change, so now there is a big change for him. Quitting his job, leaving the place he thought he would always live; but he is so excited! A true warrior and adventurer, he wants to be in Prescott with new opportunities, new digs, everything. And everyone loves him so. He will be sorely missed around here; he touches people's lives wherever he goes. He has taught me so much in such a short time, the most important being the understanding and receiving of unconditional love. I have learned that when the love is conditional, so is the forgiveness. One goes with the other, compassion being the bridge. I am able now, consciously and with much heart, to love another human being unconditionally. To experience love this way is an opportunity of a lifetime. Amen.

January 15, 1999

One more day! Bittersweet it is. I want to be home with my son, my kitty, family and friends; but to leave this magical place is difficult. For today, we go to the beach, move those silly ice cream carts, then a party for Al. Later, we'll go see Dominic at *Life's A Beach*, a bar where he plays music, and then we'll enjoy a few moments with this good man, best man at our wedding. More duties in the morning, one last deposit of stuff in the motorcycle crate, then onto the big jet airplane. Whew! Actually, at this point, a large part of me wishes it were all done, and we were quietly ensconced in the hot tub at home. But I will enjoy every minute now, and look forward to the next adventure.

Erwin in the Aspens

My Dear Aunt Amalia,

I have had the pleasure of sharing some quiet, intimate moments with Uncle Erwin this last year. There is a particular event that I want to share with you and your family.

We talked of many things together over the months: philosophies, belief systems and truth. I showed him ceremony and healing aspects of my work, how to connect with All that Is, in and around us, in a form I was taught by my dear friend, Don Américo Yábar, an Andean mystic. Mostly we meditated together or I would help him sleep. Using my "magic hands," he would say. There is a particular spot up Copper Basin, where the aspens grow in profusion around a little babbling brook, that he especially enjoyed. On a warm, somewhat cloudy day in the rainy season, we headed up to hear what the trees had to say.

Erwin was a little unsteady on his feet that day, due to the effects of chemotherapy. Because of his compromised immune system, I was especially concerned with keeping him out of the rain. I meditated while keeping one eye on the weather and the other eye on Uncle Erwin. We had been sitting quietly for fifteen minutes or so when a gentle rain began, warning us of other possibilities at that time of year. I started to get up to get Erwin back home and out of the rain, and was riveted by the beauty of this sight: there was my dear uncle, ball cap covering his bald, cold head, sitting on the ground, with his back pressed against a pine tree. With his head tilted back and his eyes closed, a soft, gentle rain washed his face and the only light in the glade showered down upon him. It was truly one of the most heavenly visions I have ever experienced. With much reluctance I broke the spell and we left our sacred site. For me, one of the greatest blessings I have in this life is this moment of beauty. All I have to do is close my eyes to be right back in the aspens with the most open person I've ever known. Maybe now that you share this vision, you can be there with me, enjoying the sounds of the wind rustling the trees as the water cascades down the little waterfall, and the Light shines on a very special man.

Mariana Speaks

Dearest Waiki,

My Aunt Mariana honored me by speaking through me for the benefit of my cousin, Chris. She is the only aspect of Spirit that speaks first person through me thus far, and that continues to be her preferred form of communication. Spirit shared deep teachings with us that day, and focused on various states of being.

April 1999

This is a reading for Chris Lytle. She wants to speak to her mother, my Aunt Mariana, who died July 6, 1996. I told her I could help.

After I entered a meditative state, Mariana simply told me to start talking, and ask Chris what she wanted. Finding it difficult to speak, Chris tearfully admitted that she wanted forgiveness for having the doctors put the breathing tube down Mariana's throat, for insisting she take the chemotherapy; in essence, for wanting her to live longer than perhaps Mariana wanted to.

"Oh no, Chris, it is I that ask for your forgiveness. I'm so sorry, I didn't really bring you up, you were more the parent. You were always stronger. I could lean on you, and I learned from you. Please forgive me for not being a very good mother." She paused and continued. "All we have is forgiveness and Love, Love and forgiveness. That is how we learn and how we grow. It is how we transform, change and learn to be."

Mariana's intent that day was to teach us about different forms of being. "It is essential you understand the reality of difference. There are different forms, spaces, dimensions, shapes and concepts, far beyond your understanding. But at the core is Love, always Love. It is Love that binds all the different beings."

"Mom, how can I help Peter?"[32]

"You must let him go; he has his own path. Unconsciously, he resents you because he perceives you as being more capable, and he is lost in his grief. He needs to grow up and stand on his own feet; I wasn't able to do that for him.

"You have to understand, Peter is a being of the Dark, the opposite of the Light. This isn't bad, it is just different and a contrast. Contrast is a constant of the universe."

She explained further, "I use the term universe loosely, as a base for your knowledge and understanding. All of the different realities are really too much for the human mind to understand. There is Dark and there is Light. I am a being of the Light. You, Chris, are of both; a yin and yang if you will, you have aspects of both. This is why sometimes you get along with Peter and sometimes you don't."

Chris mulled this over. "Ask Mom how I can be closer to her, now that she's gone . . . and in this other place."

"You must let go of all attachment. Let yourself really cry and weep. Rid yourself of your grief. I am of the Light, and where you hold that grief, I cannot enter.

"It is time for you to change now, Chris. It is a time of learning, to follow your path. This is why you are having troubles in your body. Your soul wants one thing and you are ignoring it and doing other things. The end result is like tumbling downhill—'ass over teakettle!'

"It would be good for you to pursue the Oriental beliefs, especially the Japanese. Read everything on their beliefs; search and find what feels right for you. Take the magazine *Intuition*, the copy Marilyn has with her. Take it home with you. You will find your answer in an advertisement there, when it is time."

Chris then asked about another relative with whom she was concerned. Laughing, Mariana commented that "Her type of being doesn't do well as a human. She made a mistake coming into this life as a human, and that's all there is to it!"

"What about Uncle Erwin?" I wanted to know.

"A part of him is temporarily in a sad place. This is hard for humans to understand. Many of you think that when people die, their souls go to a wonderful, happy, exalted place of incredible joy and beauty. Some do, but not all. The soul, in its own way, has sadness, and that is all a part of being. In Erwin's case, it was hard for him to leave human form; it was hard for him to leave his family."

---

32   Peter: Chris' brother.

Returning to the concept of beings, she commented that, "You, too, Marilyn, have a mistaken belief about being in the Light. You think that as you are, in human form, you can be enlightened. Not the Enlightenment the Buddha spoke of, but the feeling of, and being the Light, at all times. You are incorrect to believe that the energy and Light of Love you feel in meditation, or in your healing work, is possible at all times. It is not possible to be all Light, all the time, when you are in human form. It is our purpose in human form to advance the human condition, and advance Love and compassion in the human experience."

Taking a breath, she followed with more advice for Chris. "Chris, in order to connect with your grief, and better dispel it, spend time in the desert on a horse. You and I always connected well with horses; we understand them and they understand us."

I asked Mariana to please give my love to Grandma.[33] "Of course, she is a mother to many." I certainly know this is true; Grandma is as busy in the "ethers" as she ever was here at home. Our connection is a constant in my life.

We said our goodbyes and were at once alone. A sense of Mariana's presence, however, lasted for some time after her departure.

Mariana gave us many beautiful gifts to ponder that day, and I hope it was a help to Chris. It was certainly a help to me.

---

33   Grandma: Maziebelle Markham, Mariana's mother, who died in October 1981.

Spiritual Cake

Dear Waiki,

Al's birthday weekend was the perfect balance of quiet and busy. It seems a good example of how paying attention to each moment can make the everyday into the special, precious kind of reality it should be.

It was a sunny, busy weekend in early June 1999. Saturday morning, we attended the Lion's Pancake Breakfast to benefit the Blind Center. Great food, but not enough children present for my taste! From there we walked to the art and crafts show. I didn't care for much of it, but Al was enamored because he used to do shows like this many years ago. In the past, he worked with leather after coming home from work, then sold his belts, hats, vests and other items on the weekends. The Farmers Market was in full swing also; it just started this Saturday and will run through October. This early in the season the only fresh foods were tomatoes and onions, but there were still a lot of people checking it out. When we'd had enough, we left the downtown square and headed for home. We changed clothes, shifted gears so to speak, and left for a three-hour motorcycle trip. A perfect, warm day for a ride, we drove south. I wanted to show Al the austere beauty of Peeples Valley and Yarnell; there is so much of Arizona yet to show him! It was wonderful to be with him for such a long stretch of time, uninterrupted by work or other people. All this was followed by a luxurious nap. Somehow we squeezed in a stop at Mother's and visited with Aunt Amalia and my cousin Jim. Then back home for supper and the sanctuary of each other.

By contrast, Sunday seemed lazy and slow. Together in the quiet of my meditation room, Al and I had a remarkable healing session for his knee. Since he is connected to the energy of Jesus, that was the energy that came to help with his knee. He was told that it was really his belief and his asking for assistance from his guides and Jesus that would bring about the healing.

"Do you believe?"

"Yes," was his immediate reply. By answering as such, he was held responsible for his own healing, to rid himself of the anger that resided in his knee. I then realized all individuals are responsible for their own healing; they may require assistance from others to bring it about, but they have to take responsibility for what holds them back and for fully wanting the change. We may not always know what keeps us from moving forward, but if we set the intent to do so, that is when healing can occur.

Al was also told that we were brought together for the purpose of Love and connection, and we had teachings and meditations to do together. The simplest, most direct expression of the Love of the Cosmos is for us to love each other always, unfailing, to stand in Love and show others of our culture it can be done. It is possible to have the romantic and spiritual love linked. For two people to fully share a life, it is indeed the only way it really works.

After more meditation, we came down to earth in the cantina, discussing it all over a beer. Later we did yard work and planted flowers. To plant a garden together, to nurture it, feed it, to enjoy the bounty, it doesn't need to be any more complicated than this. Martinis finished a glorious day. You can have your spiritual and virtual cake, and eat it, too!

THREE

Connections

The Witness Athena

Dearest Waiki,

Last evening's work with Carla at her Living Wisdom Collective *was very helpful. In particular, the work with our witness. Our witness keeps us in line, so to speak. It keeps us on our Spiritual Path when we stray for any number of reasons. First we participated in a Sufi chant to prepare us for a meditation on the witness, a meditation which I found to be profound.*

In my vision, my witness was the Greek mythical Goddess, Athena. Since I was a child I have been drawn to Greek mythology, so it made sense that she would come to me now. The tall, stately goddess joined me at a gate, and took my hand so I could walk with her. At the same time that I realized who she was, she shed her warrior accouterments with the comment that she is a spiritual warrior and we no longer needed weapons in the work we were to share. As we moved forward in glowing light, there were people I was drawn to along the way, feeling the need to heal them, to assist them. She admonished me gently, asking, "When will you understand that to assist, all you have to do is radiate, to glow? You only need to be true to the work you came to do and others will be assisted in turn, simply by being in your presence." To do is not necessary; that is the teaching that I have been taught repeatedly. "It would be most helpful to flow in that direction," she kindly encouraged me.

Isn't this what you've always taught us, Waiki? The being, not the doing? We have so much to unlearn about service and our comprehension of it. We can still help and serve others as our joy and reciprocity in life. The trick is knowing there is no difference between radiating love doing our service and radiating our love through a smile, as we walk the streets of our town or take wine with our friends. It is, once again, all based on intent. The intent To Be.

The Pink Lady and Her Dog

It was Friday afternoon and I was finishing some errands when I ran into my friend Milton. A lot of time had passed since we'd visited last, so I invited him over for a beer at our cantina. Our cantina may not be what you are conjuring up. It is not a local hangout or bar where drinks are sold; it is a converted garage at the lower end of our property. It is one of the many reasons I bought the parcel in 1992. The gentleman before me enjoyed his friends and his libations, preferably together, and had taken a chain saw to the south side of the garage one afternoon, opened it up to the sunshine and filled it with all kinds of tacky and imaginative elements from Mexico, the Caribbean and Hawaii. I've heard of other pale imitators; most people seem to think it unique, and it is an engaging atmosphere for summer fun.

So, having sent Milton on his way, I finished my shopping and headed for home. I turned east onto Leroux Street; not always the most direct way home because it causes me to backtrack a block, but it is often less busy. Having just crossed Cortez Street, I was halfway between Cortez and Marina when I noticed up ahead a few pedestrians on each side of the street. I began to slow down, watching their movements, anticipating their progress to avoid any surprises.

This was the scene as I approached the intersection: On my left was a woman in matching pink polyester top and shorts, heading toward the corner. She turned slightly, looking over her right shoulder, and gave me a nod and a smile. I exchanged the same as my eyes looked beyond her to the dog walking in front of her, off leash, and about to amble across Marina Street. The dog, a big, older German Shepherd, was moving at a slight trot. Across the street from the dog were two cars at the curb, with two men and a woman involved in conversation. The dog seemed interested in checking them out. I could tell by the look of things that the dog wasn't aware of me. The owner called him, but he looked over his left shoulder instead of his right as he continued into the street. He wasn't at all aware I was present. I was now making the turn and had slowed to a crawl, knowing that when the dog finally did turn his head to the right, I would be there with my Land Cruiser. Sure enough, although with plenty of room to spare, he almost walked into the driver's door and gave me a goofy look of surprise as he changed course. I was doing no more than a mile an hour at that point.

Chuckling to myself after the encounter, I slowly began to pick up speed. In the time it took me to return my foot to the accelerator, look ahead to make sure no other cars where coming, and look in my rearview mirror to see the dog return to his owner, the pink lady and her dog were gone. Disappeared, gone without a trace. Poof! "What the hell??!!" I cried out, as I whipped around to look over my shoulder, expecting to see them next to a car at the curb, sure I had just missed them in my mirror. Not there. I braked again, scanned ahead for traffic, confused, looking in the rearview mirror and over my shoulder. Back and forth, forward, no cars, back, rearview mirror, over my shoulder, they simply were not there. I thought to myself, "They could have jumped behind the car there at the curb . . . but where are they? And *why* would they do that?" Frantic, but proceeding slowly, unsure of what I had just witnessed, I continued down the block at a very slow speed and made the right turn onto Aubrey Street toward home. Having seen nothing, the three people at the curb were still deep in conversation.

My husband Al and Milton were already there when I arrived. Their unanimous response to my experience was "Cool!"

There are times on a Spiritual Path that you may find yourself questioning the reality of the various energies, experiences and profound meditations you have. The Spiritual Path is not an easy one. There are times you're sure the best thing to do is to get a regular job, give up healing work, get back into the mainstream, and don't question what is right in front of you. I was at such a place.

I have no earthly idea why the lady and her dog entered my path nor why they left it. Maybe there was no real reason; maybe they just popped in from some other dimension and popped out just as quickly. I just happened to be there. Whether there was reason or not, and I tend to believe there is always a reason, it put me straight back on my Path, a firm believer in the magic and enormity of our beautiful universe. I no longer have any doubt that anything is possible. To quote my dear friend and mentor Cynthia Gardner, "The multiverse is a vast and mysterious place where anything is possible." So be it.

Moving With the Mountains

My Dearest Waiki,

When we started this book you told me to write about everything; the mountains, the children, the stones, any and all episodes in my life. As I proceed down this Path, many strange and wondrous things happen.

Al and I drove to Northern Arizona for an evening of camping to celebrate our second wedding anniversary and my birthday. We stayed at a lovely little lake, which was quiet because the holiday crowd had left. Our celebration went long into the night as festivities often do, and the following day we drove looking for more adventure.

We traveled through an astonishing old-growth ponderosa pine forest. Many of them are falling in number to the timber industry, but at the moment, this one is safe. What giants these were! Soaring to 80, 90 and 100 feet with a base of sometimes eight to ten feet in diameter. The forest around the pines was healthy, with many varieties of trees, nothing like you see in other places where the forest has been clear cut—cut clear of everything. Consequently, many smaller trees grow up at once, crowding each other and creating an unhealthy forest.

We enjoyed one of those magical, crystal clear days where everything flows synchronistically. All the places we were guided to were special, beautiful, serene settings we had completely to ourselves. The birds were in abundance, a few deer were seen in quiet glades, all signs telling us *Pachamama* was still in charge.

The road ended at the northernmost end of Sycamore Canyon. This is a canyon in the great Southwest tradition, steep walls of multi-hued sandstone, guarded at the top by sharp cactus with old, gnarly cedar and juniper trees. Many miles to the south, you can enter this canyon by an easy, sloping path. The stream runs most of the year, allowing you to hop rock to rock, over the fallen trees. Then you are rewarded with a small, clear pool for your warm, sweaty body. This end of the canyon, however, is severe, inhospitable to the human hiker and absolutely humbling in its ruggedness. Together we sat in silence and let the hot air roll over us. It is easy to understand how these trees have been shaped with the constant wind. Whether summer or winter, hot or cold, it is ever present, ever reminding who is really in charge.

We rambled on back the way we came, and were brought to a sudden halt as we came around a corner. A very large, open meadow spread out before us. It should have been lush from the summer rains, but they had been in short supply that summer, so the color was a blend of pale green, fading to golden. Like a Japanese sculpture garden, just a few giant pine trees flanked the meadow to give full artistic attention to the center of this simple but arresting view. There stood, with the majesty and power they command, the San Francisco Peaks.

Thrusting straight up from below, the three peaks often seem sharp and severe when seen at a distance. Today in early fall, they seemed docile and soft. Feeling their pull, we listened and felt what the great *Apus*[34] had to say in their own special, omnipotent voice. Reaching out, feeling with my hands, the peaks convey a strength of presence that contains no human thought. Just a feeling. My body swayed in time to the heartbeat of their power, back and forth; the pressure on my hands and body was alternately pulled and pushed to the rhythm of the mountains. No thought, just complete awareness of the power of the earth, humbled once again by the majesty that the All Knowing has created.

---

34   Apus: Sacred Mountains, the spirit of the mountain.

The Richness Between Life and Death

My Dearest Américo,
The ride of my lifetime, Love in the service of love, is still very much
continuing. It has been a long time since I've had the pleasure to laugh with
you and Maria up in the mountains, and I am missing my first home, Perú.

My joy here is incredible! As I mentioned before, Al and I went
ahead and got married on Maui before we went home to Arizona.
There was a lot of shock, then joy and celebration when we returned.
We had parties, talks with Morgan, and then Al was on his way back
to Maui.

Now I'll tell you something, Américo. You've said I was crazy at
times, and some might say it's crazy to agree to marry a man 48 hours
after you meet him and marry him two weeks later. But then to take
him home to meet your friends and family, and at the end of a week
put him on an airplane until you can join him in three weeks, now
that is crazy! Oh, what incredible heartache, bliss, confusion and
angst! The most beautiful part of the experience, however, was that
every time I got to tell the story of our Love, of the hand of Goddess
as she touched our hearts, I was instantly back in the moment.
Instantly in the connection, and realizing I never left. The notion that
we go somewhere else or disconnect is not accurate, is it? We just stop
paying attention. Love is always there. We just get so busy and distract-
ed we forget. It's all about remembering.

Which is what I have been falling in and out of the last few years.
The changes that I have asked for, the leaps of faith I have taken in the
service of Love have been many. It's amazing how my mind attempts
to bring me back to the seriousness of the entire world. I realized

today that it is only my mind that keeps me from Love all the time. I am perfectly capable of running my life, meeting my needs and the needs of others, and always standing in the glow of Love.

Now take Al, for example. This man is truly the meaning of service. He loves to do for others. We were discussing limousines the other day and I was saying how I would love to ride around in one. He started to speak after me, and I figured he would say something similar. But no. "I'd love to have one of those great uniforms, with the black hat and drive people around." I stood there sheepishly, nothing to say to this. The difference with Al doing service and others who say that service is their life, is that Al just *is* service. I'm so busy wasting my time talking about it. He just does it. It's nice to know there are human beings that are capable of that. It gives me hope.

Will I ever finish this letter? I think I shall just send this along and hope Arilu can translate this and you will all understand the meaning. My life is incredible, my father is ailing, my love for my family and friends is never-ending and the richness between life and death is not measurable.

Con mucho cariño,
Marylin

Everyone's Changing

The day dawns at 3:45 a.m., the day we are to leave for a vacation in Maui and my newest island, Kauai. Mostly, a funny feeling prompts me to write today. I'm not sure what; it feels like a loss. Feels like something will happen while I'm gone; someone, something large is about to change in my life. Morgan? My dad? Who?

Morgan has been down lately, primarily due to a badly turned ankle in a soccer game. It restricts his mobility. The high school soccer season is almost here and I think he wonders if he'll be able to play. When asked, he won't say; he's often difficult to read. His life is changing so rapidly, there are many things for all of us to consider. There is something indescribable about the bond between a mother and a son. Ours is such a gift; at times the rawness of it causes such beautiful pain in my soul it's hard to absorb. The inevitable separation is already in motion. Surely there must be another way for a young man to break into manhood? Seems Mom is always there. I know he doesn't take me for granted, but how can I always be there and let him move on at the same time? Does any of this make any sense? This mom stuff is hard.

Then there's my dad. Sweet, generous Dad. Since his surgeries, any walking makes him short of breath, he looks gray all the time, and often does not want any company. I suppose that's to be expected. But I'd like to ask him about that, why he wants to be so solitary. I wonder if he'd tell me. Contemplating things? His life? Future, where he's going? I will be so sad when he's gone. I'll miss him sitting on his couch that has grown soggy underneath him, the one-sided political monologues, the amazing intellect that grasps so much of the business world and translates it for the rest of us. I'll miss the ever-present TV and the pile of books. I'll especially miss the times he asked for my medical opinion. Sometimes I was able to assist and other times I had to profess ignorance. If there is a heaven, I want very much for Dad to go there; he's had his share of difficulties here on earth. Mother will be at such a loss, first because she won't have someone to complain to and mostly because, God bless her dear soul, she loves him so.

Maybe I'm the one who's changing. Old aspects of my personality are dropping away, to be replaced with I don't know what yet. A large aspect of my own spiritual healing is close at hand; I can feel it rumbling, anxious to get moving again and to assist others with theirs. That's plenty for now.

To Morgan

This was started some time ago . . . a lot about you, me, and some last minute teachings I just had to get in.

June 2, 2000

Dear Morgan,

I can really understand your anger with me and I will do my best to explain so you can hear me with your heart. My quest for love in both the romantic and spiritual world began long ago, long before you were born. I've always believed in God and a force that is all-loving and powerful. There has been a strong feeling in me that I was meant to do great works, affect and help a lot of people. Even when I was a little girl I felt this, and knew that nursing was the way I was to give. I really thought I could be the Florence Nightingale of the 20th century. I wanted to save the world and all that was in it.

So I studied hard, lost my focus a time or two, but persevered and eventually was rewarded with a degree in nursing. It was a title that said I was a registered nurse with the ability to work at my chosen career. I worked, as you know, at various aspects of nursing, which I enjoyed for many years. Then, deep inside me, stirred that which I could no longer deny.

When the unknowable stirred, I was married to your father and had you in my life. What a joy you were, as much a joy then as you are now. Every day you were filled with laughter and excitement, curious and loving. Watching you explore the world around you was, and still is the most delightful thing I have ever had the joy to encounter. The problem was that I knew I needed to end the marriage with your father in order to discover what I knew was out there for me.

This was devastating in many ways. When I married your father many people we knew looked at marriage as something that could be temporary, so if it didn't work out, they could just get a divorce. No big deal. Or live together; then it's even easier. For me, I wanted the complete commitment. I didn't want to leave at the first sign of trouble. I wanted to work it out. And I did, for many years. But I knew I needed to move forward. I needed to learn and search for a Love that I knew existed, so I could show it to you. But there was a terrible price to pay. I had to be so sure of this love that I had to be willing to give up the one thing I loved most in the world, the one person I wanted to teach and love and show love to—you.

The first few years after the divorce, every other month when you were with your father, I was full of pain, guilt and remorse. I'm sure it was no picnic for you. I busied myself, found new and crazy friends and lived a life as a single person for half the time, so as to keep my sanity.

The last three years have been especially rewarding. Since I have been willing to be the real me, which I know even in this day and age is a little weird, I feel we both have learned a lot. And speaking of learning, for the things you have taught me about my communication, both good and bad, about love that comes unconditionally, and simply being the best person I can be, I thank you. You have taught me well.

Which brings me to now. First of all, I am extraordinarily proud to be your mother. I am proud of the way you concern yourself for those less fortunate than you, and your caring nature for those who are injured or hurt. Your sense of humor! You helped me to see the humor in so many things I would have missed; you especially taught me how to laugh at myself. You were brave to take the first step and laugh at my silly ideas of importance and propriety. I was humbled and then enjoyed the laugh, too. These are enormous gifts for a child to give a parent and I am grateful, often in awe, of the determined, strong, gallant, self-respecting, loving young man that you are. You're almost not a young man anymore; you are well on your way to being a man in your own right. That is one of the advantages of age. I can see how close it is, and it is essential to tell you these things now, so you always will know what is in my heart, in the past, in the present, and in the future.

In the last year I have learned that to define what my spiritual job is, is not for me. Every time I attempt to pin down the Universe (as though that would work!) I suffer another setback with some appropriately painful lesson. I am reminded that it is enough to know that moving the energy of Love *is* my job. It is not necessary to know how it will all be manifested, what it will look like or the form it will take. This is not easy.

In our culture we are taught to have goals, plans, contingencies and, above all, know what mark we want to make on the world. Not necessarily that we want to do something important, but we're supposed to have it all worked out how we will go about it—school, career, family, how many children, retirement, eeegads! At least that's what I was taught. The problem with that paradigm is, it doesn't really leave much room for exploration. Making general plans and goals are good, but learn to be flexible if the plans change. It doesn't mean you failed; it means you weren't meant to be doing that right now. Follow the energy and listen to your heart. You seem to do that well already, and give yourself the opportunity to make many, many choices. Because all of life is choice. It is up to us to be as joyful or as miserable as we want. It is our responsibility and no one else's. The freedom you will experience, knowing you have free choice to feel good or bad, is a remarkable gift. But I digress.

As I look upon this letter, a year and one-half after I started it, it is amazing how much more true it is now than ever before. Where I was headed in this rather lengthy dissertation was to ask your forgiveness for marrying Al the way I did. It's just that we knew in the end all would turn out well and we didn't want anyone to burst our bubble at the time.

While still in Hawaii, we started to plan our wedding. Al would come home with me, then we would invite friends and family, especially you, to join us for a day filled with joy and love on September 22nd, Grandmother's birthday. Then came all the difficulties of getting everyone there. Could they come on such short notice? Where would they all stay? Could we get permission to be married in the Park? Our simple wedding was quickly turning into a logistical nightmare. We stopped laughing and everything took on such an unpleasant tone. Because we both had been married before, and we already felt that symbolically we were husband and wife, we knew we were doing the legal ceremony for our culture as a representation of our commitment to each other. We were, and always will be, completely committed to each other, with or without the piece of paper that says we were joined in marriage. We were doing the ceremony for us, not for anyone else. Maybe that was selfish on our part; maybe others would have wanted to join in on our celebration, but we figured the reality of that wouldn't be great. Everyone would have wanted us to wait, saying "What's the rush?" and all that sort of thing. Some of it I can't explain in words; it was just a feeling that the time was *now*, do it our way, this was a decision no one could make for us, no one could make for me.

As I have said before, my only regret, and it's a big one, is that you weren't there. It was indeed a lousy choice I offered you. Only giving you the choice to be in the wedding or not, and not have any other say, was definitely lousy. It was really an impossible choice I gave you when I called you from Hawaii and, again, I apologize. As you know, I just couldn't have you hear that I was getting married from anyone else and my hand was forced. I shall forever be saddened that I had to make that phone call, because I knew, even though I secretly hoped otherwise, what your answer would be.

Two things I want to reiterate here. One: If you ever have a big decision to make, a decision that most people wouldn't consider, or a career path that some can't understand, if you know in your heart of hearts it's the right choice for *you* because it feels like nothing you've ever experienced before and it feels *so right*, by all means go forth and do it! You are the only one who can ultimately make your own decisions because you are the only one who will live the consequences to the fullest. And I do mean the fullest. There are some decisions we make that *do* involve others; those are the ones for which we must deeply search our hearts. And believe me, I searched very hard and deep concerning my marriage to Al.

Okay, now two: I know I've said this before, but I want it in writing, so you know what a strong desire it still is in my life. I would give *anything* to have you at our marriage ceremony. To have the chance to renew our vows, with you there this time, I will never stop wanting. It may sound like "Oh, well, its just a renewal," but that's not it at all. It would be completely different to have you there, a bonding and union that I cheated myself and you out of before. So please hold this in your heart, and if and when you're ready, we'll have a beautiful day. It may be many years from now. But just know I always hold it in my heart to complete the union that Al and I began on September 4, 1998, but felt incomplete because I couldn't have you there. I see as I write this, it is time to forgive myself, as I also ask you to forgive me.

The relationship you and Al are beginning to form, the always shifting relationship with me as I learn to let go of you, all of this, and watching you grow into a man, is a wondrous, beautiful thing. It is with true pleasure, many tears and just a slight bit of angst (Did I tell him everything? Did I finish my job? Have I done it well?) that I set you out into the world. Go forth and know how proud I am of you and how I love who you have grown up to be. I will always be here and available for you, should you want to come in from the cold or just want a bit of tenderness and advice.

On this Graduation Day, June 2, 2000, know I love you with the fullest of my being and I thank you for being such a kind and gentle teacher.

All my love,
Mom

Mazie in Her Glen

My Waiki,

My sweet Aunt Mazie, who encouraged me as a writer, died this summer, in July 2000. I had a vision of her while she lay dying, happy and at peace riding a beautiful horse. She always did love horses.

A bit of prose for you, Aunt Mazie, this vision came to me recently in meditation.

The palomino mare races across the verdant meadow; as she slows we notice the bluebells, the honeysuckle, thistle and wild mustard. The sun is high overhead in the middle of a cloudless sky; summer is in full bloom. The bees buzz their constant drone while the sun bores down with unrelenting heat. There is a young girl on the horse's back, with flaxen hair like the pony's. Her tresses stream behind her, long ago having lost the ribbon meant to hold them in check. Her eyes wide and her mouth in a perpetual smile, horse and rider seem anatomically as one. They slacken to a trot as they reach the forest's edge. Stopping to appreciate the cool moistness of the trees, reverently the mistress slides from the mare's back. As if on tiptoe, they enter the sacred space together, sure of the route, footpath green and quiet with its covering of mossy undergrowth.

Dappled light dances on the forest floor as the breeze touches the treetops, assurance to the pair they are welcome. Faintly at first, building to a quiet crescendo, the sound of the small waterfall floats toward them, beckoning. Once in the glen, the routine long ago established, the mare bends her head to nibble the tall grass as the young lady sensuously moves toward the icy water, bright sun engulfing the open glade. Having discarded her clothes in this private sanctuary, she allows the hot sun to play on her bare, young breasts and belly. She floats lazily on her back, listening to the water from above join the pool below. She is home.

May you enter your own sanctuary soon, the pain of your present existence left far behind.

Much love,
Marilyn

Death Waits for Us All

My Dear Waiki,

Death swirls around me as a black, wispy fog. I have chosen a work of death and grieving. I set myself in front of death to assist others through the trauma; still, the bell that tolls in me of the sadness of loss is great. My father will die soon, a loving aunt is gone, a young man too soon is lost, the sweet laughter and stories of our friends and families all too soon will be lost to us forever. All gone, including us. It weighs heavily sometimes, this grief. I feel the weight of a family's grief right now, although I'm sure I cannot know the true magnitude of their feelings. To watch a younger sister left behind, blind to the world, unable to comprehend a world without her big brother, her best friend, to guide her, it is more than I can bear. The mourners, the family, unable to understand how such a bright flame is so quickly put out—we stand mute in front of the inevitable. Desperately we search out familiar faces, hoping to ease the pain and encroaching fear that this could be us; this could be our death, or worse yet, this could be our child, cut down just as we were really beginning to know them. No, not that.

My worst nightmare is this: my son gone from me at the age of 21. Maybe if I finally get it down on paper I can let it go. I had a vision once and couldn't see Morgan past the age of 21. I panicked. I rationalized. I chose not to give it any thought, I blocked the drama from my mind. That was five years ago. He is eighteen now. Periodically it would slip into focus; quickly I moved my mind to something else. Occasionally I would allow myself to linger on this premonition—maybe it just meant that who or what I saw Morgan as being would be substantially different after 21 years of age. That's it! Or so I have led myself to believe. I now visualize what he might look like much later in life, grown, family, with children of his own. I don't know if I'm fooling myself or comforting myself, it doesn't much matter. There are some things a parent just can't or isn't supposed to see. I figure this is one of them. Death. It comes to us all, like it or not, when we're least expecting it. Go and live. Carpe Diem.

Making Room for More

Dear Waiki,

An unusual meditation and channeling took place recently. Considering the Q'ero beliefs and prophecies, I believe you will find it interesting.

My friend Ramona and I spend a few hours together every week discussing various spiritual topics and enjoying meditations together. During one of our sessions, we were discussing the vast numbers of people who were dying—many artists, writers, and famous people who had made a large impact on the world in their lifetime. In a moment of quiet contemplation, looking out the window at nothing, I began to speak from a place of wisdom that was unknown to me, speaking with power, clarity and determination.

"Yes, there are many souls leaving the planet at this time," I began. "The reason for this is to make more room for others to come in. These individuals that have left have done so willingly. What is needed here is a change in awareness. To know when one's job here is done, is the beginning. Then, to be willing to leave when you have fulfilled your plan for a lifetime, is the next step. This then allows more room, if you will, for the next, more aware souls to enter. This creates more balance. As it is now, you hold on to life, thinking it the end-all, fearing there is nothing more beyond this life as you know it. In the meantime, more souls are entering and it is getting literally crowded. So, to know your own plan here is essential; then you will know when it is completed, and be willing to leave and move forward in your evolutionary and spiritual path. We are curious to see if you (as a species) can create this balance. It is possible; this can be achieved. We offer you the choice. We are curious to see if you will take this challenge or continue to dominate the limited world in which you live and then go on to dominate and pollute more of the worlds around you in your quest for more, when less is possible. Can you do this?"

My gaze shifted back to Ramona as I settled into my comfortable chair. We sat in silence, wondering about the interesting challenge we had been offered.

Hatred

Mi Querido Waiki,

It has taken quite a while to write this particular letter. I have experienced the energy of hatred and fear and have found it most difficult to resume my Pollyanna ways. I remember your discussions of brujas[35] *and the* kuti-kuti *ceremony to remove malevolent energy from others. I didn't believe it existed. I felt at the time these discussions were more symbolic than literal, due to the fact you often taught in parables and stories, and frankly, I didn't believe you. I've changed my mind.*

On a fine, starry evening in the middle of November 2000, I had a taste of real fear and was shown the strength and power of Love and prayer. "Fear is the absence of Love." These words of yours, describing a perpetual human condition, held me up and helped me overcome an indefinable evil.

I was relishing the last few minutes alone in the hot tub before I retired for a meditation prior to bed. Having just settled in, the water almost to my nose for the fullest effect, I took a deep breath, and surrendered to the heat and the nothingness of thought. Hardly a moment had passed, barely enough to fully relax, when a loud, eerie, tap, tap, tap began on the cover of the spa. I had folded back one half of the cover; there was no need for more. Startled, I sat up, reassuring myself it was the thermometer, trapped between some layers; it was only audible because of the movement of the water. The problem with that conclusion was that the water had not been moving; it was perfectly still. The tapping continued, louder now, moving in my direction. To say I was terrified would be an understatement. I don't recall ever being so frightened. I knew I must get the upper hand, show no fear, as the tapping grew more insistent and I backed out of the water. "Fear is the absence of Love!" I proclaimed loudly. Thinking of you and the effects of shifting energy, all I could do was to growl in

35   bruja: a witch.

a very base manner, pulling from my gut all the fury, size and strength I could muster. To be bigger, more vicious, more dangerous, than what was in that water; that was what I had to do. To give over to fear and run was not an option. If that had been my choice, my life would have been altered irreparably and my Spiritual Path would be ruled by fear and chaos. Somehow, I knew this in just a few seconds of thought, and my choice was to stand firm. Moving swiftly, I flung the cover shut, and shaking, I latched it. The tapping grew louder still, the sound having moved now to where I had been sitting not thirty seconds before. I stood my ground, the noise now in the corner of the tub, still batting at the cover, fighting for release. I was sure it could shoot out any second at me. "No! I will not give in!" I shouted, bravely. Frantically searching for a prayer, I suddenly hit on *The Prayer of St. Francis*. "Oh Lord, let me be an instrument of your peace." The tapping slowed ever so much. "Where there is hatred, let me sow love." It slowed markedly then.

I continued with "Where there is injury, pardon," and so on, to the completion of the prayer. By the time I was done, the tapping had ceased. The energy, however, had not dissipated. With a terrific amount of terror still in my heart, I spoke angrily and forcefully to the entity as I strode to my meditation room to turn off the heat and put out the light. This caused me another moment of fright, as I had to walk the length of the room in darkness. Determined not to be beaten, I moved forward, claiming my space for myself only. Praying aloud, speaking of the sanctity of my home and my sanctuary, I made my way out of the room and up the stairs. "I have the Light and Jesus at my side! You can never overpower me! You cannot overcome the Warrior Spirit!" From the landing with even more vigor, I announced to the being that my sanctuary was surrounded by white jaguars, guardians of my home and my Spirit, and it would not beat me with fear. "I know what you are, and you will not push me from my place or my Path! I am stronger! I live in the arms of Love, in God, in all that is wonderful and good in the Universe! You will go back from whence you came! I have powerful, Love-filled assistants, and we stand firm with Love at our disposal—I will have no fear as 'Fear is the absence of Love'!" Being further away certainly gave me more courage. I stood my ground and yelled at it to leave. With the utmost indignation, I turned and stomped into the house. Slamming the door, I closed out the horror.

The rest of the evening was restless for me as I continued to say prayers, knowing this was not a guide trying to get my attention. My cat Mikay, who always goes outside with me, had not returned. Not allowing myself to be scared for her, I visualized her at my feet, curled up and sleeping soundly on the bed. I couldn't even speak of my encounter to my husband Al, not wanting to recreate any energy around it. Eventually, Mikay came running in the house, dashing from room to room, tail puffed, as if the literal Devil was on her heels. She refused to settle down until I finally climbed back into bed; then she jumped on the blanket and settled down to sleep in the exact spot I had visualized for her safety.

A lot of contemplation and meditation went into this experience the following week. Finally I spoke to Al of my ordeal and then did as he suggested, which was to "get back on that horse," and enjoy my hot tub once again. I realized that for years I had never really believed in evil, thinking it a manifestation of the human condition. What I had felt and heard that night was evil of a kind; hatred, plain and simple. That's why *The Prayer of St. Francis* was the right one to dissipate it, with the second line being "Where there is hatred, let me sow Love." I knew that when I uttered that line I had hit on the correct theme, and, as Paul Harvey, a national radio commentator, says, "And now—for the rest of the story . . . ."

Before I went to sleep that same evening, I stowed my rosary under my pillow and turned on my side, wanting to feel safe and secure. In doing so, I squished my earrings into the pillow, having forgotten to take them off. I removed them, setting them on my bedside table. What I know to be true is that all of these experiences, all of these manifestations of God, be they Love, Hate, Beauty, Horror, Death, Charity, Filth or Disease, are all expressions of the One. So I wasn't too surprised the next morning (albeit I did search everywhere) when only one of my earrings remained—one of a pair, in the shape of a heart. It's all the same thing, "everything's everything," to quote Mark P. Duke. Perhaps the hatred I experienced just needed to know infinite Love and Strength. I hope that in me, it found its expression fulfilled.

Tom's Rebirth

You know, Waiki, there are many strange things that happen in the Universe that have no explanation. You can look at them from all kinds of viewpoints and still not have a satisfactory answer. Occasionally, if you're lucky, you find an explanation you can live with.

I had an important dream the other night about our friend and waiki, Tom Best. You were also in the dream. We were conducting a workshop and when it was over and the participants had left, I heard your voices coming from a room off a sunny, enclosed patio. Following the sound of talk and laughter, I sought out the two of you. I entered the room to find not you, but Tom talking with a group I didn't recognize. They seemed none too pleased by my interruption. Tom and I moved off from the group so I could give him something special I was holding. It was a beautiful, white, somewhat translucent stone carved in bas relief, the size of my palm. My tone had shifted from one of gaiety to solemnity as I gave him the stone.

"You take this with you when you leave, wherever you're going."

He admired the stone and thanked me for it. That was all, that was the end of the dream. It caught my attention, however, because it was so strong and I could see and remember every detail. The pink color of the sandstone on the patio, the warmth of the air as it caressed my face while I followed the voices, and the white stone. The stone was cool to the touch, with a large X carved out of the rock on one side and a very, feminine, curvy design on the other.

The next day, I was driving to my sister's new house to help with some moving-in chores. I was in a fine mood and looking forward to seeing her new home. Contemplating the dream, wondering why it seemed so strong, I heard a song on the radio. It was one I had always wanted Tom to hear. He was always making me listen to various pieces of music, to hear the significance of a particular song. As I listened to this favorite piece, I thought, "Dang it! I always wanted Tom to listen to this song!"

Suddenly, with a flash of urgency the two pieces came together. First the dream with the stone and my accompanying comment about him taking it with him. Then the song, and my feeling that he would never hear it. Swiftly it felt like something dreadful had happened to Tom.

As you know, Tom and Bobbi moved to San Antonio 18 months ago. Many people discount coincidences as being just that, but that's not been my experience. Feeling as if some very bad news had just come my way, I began to shake, and was grateful for the turnoff ahead so I could get off the main road. In tears, feeling as if I'd lost a best friend, I jerked the car to the side of the road, pulled to a stop, and gave in to the wailing sobs that began to rack my body, in disbelief that I could be experiencing such a thing with no clear knowledge that something had happened to Tom. But I felt it in the core of my body, while my mind argued, "No! I was sure I'd see you again, Tommy!" "No! You don't know this to be true!" I told myself. Many thoughts ran back and forth as I tried to calm myself so I could check in, to see if I could get some kind of an energetic answer.

". . . just here differently, you can always talk to me . . ." came the jumbled reply.

Now, there is something you must know, Waiki. I have been doing the best I can to leave the world of drama behind, not wanting to live in that world of ego. This was incredibly real, just as if someone had called me on the phone to tell me. There was the briefest moment where it felt very similar to the grief I experienced when my guide Mort left me, when you and I began our work together. Choking back the sobs after I had let myself bawl, I began to think outside my own grief, to Bobbi's. This propelled me to the phone to discover the truth.

After more tense moments, I got Bobbi on the phone and she assured me Tom was not only not dead, but doing very well, indeed.

"You better check your psychic connection, Marilyn! Tom's just fine!"

Tom came in a few minutes later and she handed him the phone. It was so good to hear his voice! I told him that when he really does die, I probably won't grieve as much, having already gone through that today. He was very understanding and didn't tease me; just listened as I told him the story and appreciated both my grief and concern. We visited more with appropriate amusement, now that I could laugh, and promised to stay in touch.

I ruminated about my experience that evening and the following day, and remembered the aspect of my grief that felt so similar to Mort's parting. I recalled a conversation I had with Tom a couple of years ago, discussing the available energetic connection of the waikis of the mountains of Perú, the *Q'ero* Indians.

"The thing that I really like about the waikis, Tom, is they're always there! It's like you can pick up a telephone and call them. They're always available to help with healing, cleaning, or just a felt presence."

"Yeah," he replied, "I've always wondered what part of their spirit are we getting? Is it the real-time aspect or simply a facet of themselves that they always make available to us?"

"Yes, I wonder." We moved to silence, contemplating the possibilities.

Suddenly, something clicked. I think what I felt that day driving was not so much a true death, but a symbolic one. It was Tom's spirit way of saying, "Go ahead, now, you're in good hands, you're on your own. You'll be just fine." His teaching had ended and it was time to enjoy his friendship, to enjoy a relationship that was based on equal footing, as opposed to teacher-student. It was time to use his teachings for my service for all beings. I'm at peace and he has been reborn.

The Discipline of Meditation

When learning meditation, there are many teachers who will tell you that discipline is very important. I happen to one of them. Choose the same place every day, the same time, a place with lots of peace and quiet. Create a space just for this if possible; create an altar there also, a place for spiritual objects, things that matter to you, that have significance. There are many methods of meditating. You can focus on the breath, a mantra, a prayer, anything that will create a quietness of mind and body. Some people like to listen to guided meditations on tape, and there are a great many of these available today. As with any practice, the most important thing is consistency and discipline.

The Eastern tradition generally recommends meditation first thing in the morning for about a half-hour, then in the evening also if you can. This is ideal for people who wake easily in the morning, but not so good if the tendency is to fall asleep. In this country, with no real tradition to follow in regard to meditation, many Americans follow the suggestions of the Eastern religions without heeding their own biorhythms. The problem can be this: You want to learn to meditate, or even know how, but want to add a new dimension to your meditative path. In the past you have had a routine of getting up in the morning, maybe writing, reading or engaging in exercise. Then, if time allows and you don't have any immediate appointments, you do your meditation.

However, in the real world, you have things to accomplish, clients to see, shopping to do, a job to go to and, before you know it, the day is done and you haven't done your meditation. So, at five o'clock in the afternoon, you spend a half-hour in meditation and continue with your evening. Is this a problem? No! The point is to get the meditation in. Now, if you are just beginning, it is best to choose a certain time of day and follow that for quite some time until you get the hang of it. But your certain time of the day and someone else's may be different. If you are feeling resistance to doing the meditation every day because you "should," by all means step back and address why you are finding resistance. There are many possibilities for this, but what I would suggest is to meditate on it to discover what it may be! Your own inner voice will help you along; trust what it tells you. Maybe it's the method, the time of day, or just plain resistance to being told you "should" do it a certain way. Of course, there may be a change in your life you are feeling resistance to; spiritual practice reveals aspects of our lives so we may see them more clearly. This is why meditating on the answer is so important.

If you want to meditate to find answers, inner peace and quiet, you will find your own way to the Silence, in your own time, and at your own pace.

Ahimsa

My dear Yoga teacher, Sally Cheney, is always adding different spiritual aspects to our Kripalu Yoga practice. Today she introduced us to the *Yamas* and *Niyamas*, the two aspects of the eight limbs of Ashtanga Yoga. This is the summary she provided:

The ancient sage Patanjali was the first to systematize the practices of Ashtanga Yoga. Yoga literally means "union." Through stilling the mind, union with our divine source is achieved. Practices of Yoga (sadhana) purify the body and the mind for the purpose of developing concentration. Concentration brings us to a knowledge of reality and inner peace.

The eight limbs of Ashtanga Yoga are: *Yama* (restraints), *Niyama* (observances), *Asana* (posture), *Pranayama* (control of prana or breath), *Pratyahara* (withdrawing the mind from the senses), *Dharana* (concentration), *Dhyana* (meditation) and *Samadhi* (enlightenment).

Kripalu Yoga incorporates the last six limbs into posture practice, thus becoming a practice of "meditation in motion." However, any complete yoga practice continues off the mat, and the *Yamas* and *Niyamas* help guide us in our everyday lives to deepen our awareness of who we are and how we are "being" with our brothers and sisters so that life becomes a more enriching experience for us all.

Yamas (Restraints)

Ahimsa: Nonviolence. To refrain from causing pain, either mental or physical, to any living being, including oneself.

Satya: Truthfulness. To develop honesty; to avoid deceiving others and oneself.

Asteya: Nonstealing. To avoid any kind of misappropriation of material or nonmaterial things, such as acceptance of undeserved praise.

Brahmacharya: Continence. To conserve and redirect the sexual
    energy. Literally translated, it means "To walk on God's path."
    Sexual energy is redirected into works that benefit one's fellow
    man.
Aparigraha: Nonhoarding. To avoid the accumulation of unneces-
    sary possessions. To free ourselves from attachment to material
    things.

Niyamas (Observances)
Shaucha: Purity. Cleanliness of the body and purity of the mind.
Santosha: Contentment. More than a passive state of mind,
    contentment is a virtue to be actively cultivated in order to
    free the mind from the effects of pleasure and pain.
Tapas: Austerity. Literally, "to burn." Implies the burning of all
    desires by means of discipline, purification and penance in
    order to gain control over the body and senses.
Svadhyaya: Scriptural study. The study of scriptures, self-inquiry
    and liberation through studying the lives and teachings of
    saints and association with spiritually minded people.
Ishvarapranidhana: Surrender to God. Recognition that the limited
    ego-self is an illusion; channeling of energies toward the
    realization of truth, or God.
"Do your work by surrendering to God. Don't think that you are
    helping others, but think that God is helping them, taking you
    as his instrument."
"The aim in life is to attain peace. No one can give us peace. We
    can't buy or borrow it. We have to cultivate it by practicing
    Yama and *Niyama*."[36]

To give us something to focus on for the day, Sally read these
aloud before we started our yoga practice. Immediately I was drawn to
Ahimsa, nonviolence. I felt a joy rise up in me and knew intuitively
that if you mastered one, you mastered them all. It wasn't that I
thought I could, just that I knew this was the truth. Indeed, that was
the next comment Sally made, although her term was Enlightenment.
She next challenged us to focus on one of these practices for the next
few weeks and see what happened.

Because I am a spiritual being having a human experience, my ego
and doubt had been in the way lately. On that very evening of my

36   Dass, Baba Hari. *Ashtanga Yoga Primer*. Sri Rama Publishing, 1981.

yoga class, as I was driving to a restaurant, I provided myself with a lot of "I should be getting up at six o'clock in the morning and meditating!" "I slept in again! I'm worthless! I have no discipline!" and other variations on the worthless theme. In other words, being human.

Sitting at a stop light, I was caught up in this self-abuse. Suddenly, in front of me, in large, bright, primary colors, the word AHIMSA appeared! The letters flashed brightly off and on like a neon sign. In a flood of shimmering light, tenderness and dazzling awareness of everything around me, I realized what I had been doing. The tears rolled down my cheeks as I began to laugh and cry, affirming aloud, "Ahimsa! Ahimsa!" My world was filled with an unutterable sense of awe and peace. I was the last person in the world I wanted to hurt, to inflict violence upon, and I realized what a hurtful thing I had been doing. To tear myself down so, to belittle myself when all I really want to do in life is be God's instrument of Love and joy!

The following days were filled with a deep sense of relief. I shifted my energy and returned to the Path of doing for others as I do for myself. If I can't be kind to myself, how on earth can I be kind to others? The answer is of course, I can't. It always comes back to self. If we are to care for others, we must first take care of ourselves.

God in the Mirror

It was my turn to choose a topic for our meditation group one evening, so I brought a number of ideas, including a summary of *Yamas* and *Niyamas* my yoga teacher had given me. We decided to each choose one and focus on it in meditation. Having had some experience in the last few weeks with the *Yama, Ahimsa,* I chose to focus on the *Niyama, Ishvarapranidhana,* or more simply, surrender to God.

My brain swirled a bit as it often does at the beginning of meditation, quieting the internal dialogue, as my mind focused on my last thought, which was the word prayer.

"Prayer" and "God" soon became one, then "God" became my mantra for the meditation. I had that curious sensation of feeling somehow light and heavy at the same time, while the gentle music in the background occasionally entered my awareness. God was all around me, in me, everywhere. As I had done earlier that evening, I saw myself looking in the mirror, feeling God everywhere. Suddenly it was very bright in the room, however, I know the light never changed. I was observing an intangible light. Then, as I looked into the mirror of my memory and watched myself fuss with my hair, being critical as I scrutinized, I realized I was also looking at God. Here I was looking at God—that which is in me always—and being critical! A pleasant shift took place then, as I laughed at and to myself, and sat in the realization of God within me, knowing it would indeed be difficult to be so critical again.

Reflections on Reality

Dearest Waiki,

   I offer one of my many contemplations on reality. It is a gift to know these "thoughts" don't just come from my own mind, but the collective mind of All. Enjoy!

If we believe in the basic premise of reincarnation, wherein we continue to come back and learn and take care of karma, we are always in the human experience, reaching toward Enlightenment.

If we understand the veil is just as close as you and I, sitting here together, we can learn that we can go directly to the other side and remember it all, use it all.

I have chosen to be here in this physical plane, but can travel to many different realities and dimensions at will, with the firm knowledge that my body is still here in this existence. The purpose is to learn and teach of the myriad possibilities. Then, when I do pass over to the next reality, I can take that learning with me.

We need never forget, but know we have taught others before us and will continue to do so, either in this plane or another reality or dimension. The goal is to teach others in this reality the process of remembering, reconnecting and relearning. To go beyond God. For me, it is instructive to teach others about these possibilities so they may better follow their own path. For myself, it is so I may continue to do my work of Love in as many ways as possible—and the possibilities appear to be extremely vast.

The Dalai Lama's Practice

Dear Waiki,

I wanted to include this practice I received in my e-mail because this is how I try to lead my life, and because I had the honor to spend four days in California in His Holiness the Dalai Lama's presence, hearing him teach on The Heart of Wisdom *sutra. I was so touched by his humility, and would like to honor His Holiness by sharing this with as many people as possible.*

We heard recently from someone who returned from India. Her group met with the Dalai Lama for several days. The meetings focused on dialoguing what they believed were the five most important questions to be considered moving into the new millennium.

The group was asked to come up with five questions before meeting with the Dalai Lama. They asked:

"How do we address the widening gap between rich and poor?"

"How do we protect the earth?"

"How do we educate our children?"

"How do we help Tibet and other oppressed countries and peoples?"

"How do we bring spirituality—deep caring for each other—through all disciplines?"

"All the questions fall under the last one," the Dalai Lama said. "If we have true compassion our children will be educated, we will care for the earth and for those who 'have not.'"

He then asked the group, "Do you think loving on the planet is increasing or staying the same?" "My experience," he responded to his own question, "leads me to believe that love IS increasing."

He shared a practice with the group that will increase loving and compassion in the world, and asked everyone attending to go home and share it with as many people as possible.

The Practice:

1. Spend five minutes at the beginning of each day remembering we all want the same thing (to be happy and loved) and we are all connected.
2. Spend five minutes cherishing yourself and others. Let go of judgments. Breathe in cherishing yourself, and breathe out cherishing others. If the faces of people you are having difficulty with appear, cherish them as well.
3. During the day, extend that attitude to everyone you meet; we are all the same, and I cherish myself and you. Do this with the grocery store clerk, the client, your family, coworkers, etc.

Stay in the practice, no matter what happens.

That's the trick, no matter what happens.

Why I Do the Work

Dearest Waiki,

Working with a young woman recently, one of the real joys of this work came to me and I want to share it with you. She was a tentative, quiet woman in the process of putting together a commune, and felt as if she was running into obstacles. She was anxious to get under way and everyday felt like a setback. I explained to her that I worked quietly, sometimes talking, and would move my stones and hands over both her physical and energetic body.

As I began, I was drawn to her head and held it in my hands. I did not speak, just sent quiet, calming light into her mind, as her thoughts had the tendency to overwhelm her. She was so full of mental dialogue, I energetically relaxed her mind. As my hands engaged in the energy, with sweeping movements, I whisked the thoughts away, cleaning, making her head empty. Moving around to the right side of her, my stones were laid out on the *mesa*. I'd already given her my purple amethyst to hold in her pocket for "little boy energy."[37] Drawn to her heart, with one of my stones, I began cleaning the area as Spirit began to speak.

I saw a little girl, I told her, standing on the side of the road. She is about two years old and crying. She's been left and she feels completely alone. In this child's mind she *is* all alone. She doesn't know someone is coming back for her; she was sure she had been left for good. The sense of loss is acute.

"This is what you carry with you now, this sense of aloneness, and the desire for community. The reason the commune won't come together right now is that you must clear these issues up for yourself so the community you desire will be a whole, healthy family, not a desire for the illusory family of your dreams that didn't happen."

---

37   little boy energy: the amethyst I carry was given me by my son to keep me safe on my first trip to Perú.

She nods. Her son is 18 months old. It is due to the proximity of the boy's age to hers when she had this experience, that she feels the acuteness of this loss and desires to banish the emptiness from her soul. But in the process of attempting to create this physical place of community, she has not let anyone into her heart. Sweeping and moving loving energy with my breath toward her heart, I assisted her to be more open with others. I suggested she treat her heart like a zipper, open it notch by notch, and if it gets too scary she can quickly close it back up, then reopen it. Moving on to her stomach, drawn to the area, I sensed her discomfort. Spirit told her to follow her own intuition, to use her knowledge of diet and foods to eat what her own body wanted. She was to learn to meditate and listen to what her body needed.

As I was finishing, a sense of death and loss came to me. I asked her if she had lost anyone . . . in the last six months? No words came out, but the tears did. Her body began to shake as she attempted to keep the sorrow in. Reassuring her, I encouraged her to cry. It was obvious she had little experience in that; she kept a strong rein on her emotions. Here again Spirit encouraged her to release these emotions, learn to express them; otherwise, they would cause problems with her stomach. Sensing that is where her stress was centered, I communicated that to her.

The session was coming to a close, and I knew this had been exhausting for her. She would need extra energy to get home safely. I moved above her head, chanting as you have taught me. *Hamqui espíritu, hamqui espíritu*, calling her name, blowing into the top of her head. Energizing her, seeing her inner candle of *ánimu*[38] grow larger as I breathed more life into her, I felt her energy increase. I leaned back on my heels to see her open her eyes as she grinned up at me with childlike abandon.

This is why I do the work. She sat up and we hugged, she being grateful for the motherly attention, I loving the ability to be of service and see her shine.

---

38   *ánimu*: the life force enters your crown at birth and leaves the same way at death. Performing hamqui for another person increases their vital force, and thus their energy.

Letting Go of Mariana

I flew to Los Angeles Saturday morning to say goodbye to Estelle. She was an elderly friend of my family's; she had suffered a stroke on Monday. Estelle had been my grandmother's personal secretary for 25 years. She began her employment at the time of my birth. Because of this, we'd always had a special bond. She was now in a coma and not expected to live more than a few days.

I had little time to contemplate her or our shared memories once I was on the freeway headed south to Laguna Beach. It took all my senses to stay alive with the speeding cars whipping around me. I did have a specific need to see her, though. Both my grandmothers died before I could say goodbye, and I never really knew my grandfathers. This was the urgency to my trip; it was selfish and completely for me. Because of her stroke, I was told there was only a slight chance she would know I was there. I needed this connection, not she.

I arrived at Victor and Estelle's home midafternoon and there was Vic, waiting for me. He sat motionless, staring into his memories, ready to take another trip to Estelle's bedside. Now in a nursing home, there was no need for a hospital for Estelle; she only needed a place to die. Vic was too old to care for her himself; this had been his only choice. We said hello and hugged, and he told me how much he appreciated my coming all this way. Memories came flooding into my mind, as I remembered days at the beach enjoyed long ago, with card games over a smoky table, and lots and lots of laughter. Vic didn't look all that different to me now, even at the age of 88. I always called him "my Jack La Lanne." He always seemed tan and strong; with hardly a gray hair in his head. But as I looked closer, he *had* changed, and seemed smaller without Estelle.

For the next three days, Victor and I visited with Estelle, talking as if she could hear us, and I documented the stories Victor shared with me. We had a good many laughs (Estelle would've liked that), and a good many tears. Without knowing it, I was drawing Victor out, reassuring him that he'd done everything he could, while listening to him pour out his heart for his lady love. In the end it was work, a work I'm good at, and I'm grateful for my ability.

Later in meditation at my hotel, I asked Estelle if there was anything we could do for her. Was there anything she needed? Could I tell Vic anything for her?

"Tell him I really liked the boat ride, I really liked the boat. And be sure to tell him I love him."

Since they'd been married 54 years, this was especially poignant, but with Estelle's impending death, Vic's self-doubts had begun to resurface. She was his world, his strength, his rock. He wondered how he would get along without her.

I did question her twice in meditation about the remark concerning the boat. She assured me that was what she wanted me to say and, later in her room, in response to my question again, she moved her foot at the time I indicated. So I plunged ahead, telling Vic that sometimes I was able to hear Spirit in a way others could not and Estelle had something specific to tell him.

"She said to tell you she really liked the boat ride, she really liked the boat." I've learned not to paraphrase, Spirit is always specific. "I'm not sure what this means, Vic."

He did, however. "Oh! Well, I had a little sailboat that we'd take over to Catalina at times, then there was the cruise ship we took twice to Hawaii. Oh, yes, Estelle was quite the sailor, she really loved that sailboat." He then proceeded to regale me with many stories of their trips to Hawaii, the all-night dancing and the romance of it all. I finished by telling him she did indeed love him. "Apparently so . . . ." was his sad response.

Later, I took my leave of them both, crying as I told Estelle how much I loved her and begging her to go now, as this kind of living was so hard on Vic. There was nothing else to do but wait for Estelle to take her final breath.

I drove down the coast to the beach and spent two hours with my toes in the sand, listening to the surf. I did not cry for Estelle; she would be free soon. Quietly and with intent, I invited the wind and the sea to cleanse me of my sorrow.

That evening, my friend Linda and I sat discussing the spiritual nature of things, especially death, as it was so near. I mentioned there was need in our culture to cultivate a willingness for death and transformation when a person's spiritual work is done. To know when that time is and leave without fear; knowing there is another reality elsewhere and more opportunities to live our soul's purpose. It would be wonderful for all of us to slip our earthly bonds when we accomplished our spiritual life's goals, leaving room for more souls to enter, and then move on.

The next morning, the opposite side of that possibility was shown to me. There, on the counter in the bathroom, far away from my purse, was the little gold starfish that had been hooked on the purse just the evening before. The purse had belonged to Mariana, my dear aunt in whose house I was presently staying. She had died four years previously. "Why do you do this?" I inquired of her. "I believe you're here . . . ."

Then I realized what she was telling me. If people are willing to leave this earth and go to another reality, then the living must be willing to let them go. I've always cherished knowing that Aunt Mariana and Grandma have kept such a good eye on me, reassuring me on my Path, consoling me when in doubt and boosting my Faith in the All Knowing. But even in death, not wanting them to be completely gone, I have held them close. It was time; they had other things to do.

At that moment of realization, knowing that Spirit is available to all of us, my Faith in The One was strengthened. We do not need individual spirit to reassure us, we need only ask of the Great Spirit. That which is all around us, within us, that which is The Unnameable, that which is Yahweh, that which is God. This is the only Spirit we ever truly need address. It simply takes us coming full circle to see what has been in front of us all along. So simple, yet so difficult. With much love and poignant sorrow, I left the little starfish on the counter and hoped it would assist Mariana on her Way.

The Love For My Mother

My Dear Américo,

This is a disjointed rambling from me today. My mother had a small stroke in early January of 2001, and it gave me quite a fright, along with a reminder of the preciousness of life.

It began with Mother having some difficulty writing, a dropped glass, and then problems with her speech and finding the correct words to express herself. I believe the most frustrating and scary thing for her was the inability to say what she knew was in her mind or not recognizing that what she said didn't make sense. She is an editor, a writer and my proofreader, and loves the play and use of words. Mother is the keeper of the English language; that is what it seems to all who know her! To be unable to express herself in speech was especially frightening.

What was it like for me? The temporary loss of the strong, dynamic woman that is my mother was difficult to comprehend. The loss of the expectation that she would live forever or that she would die sometime after my father. That's normal, right? To be expected, right? But there is no normal, there is no expected. She might actually die before my father. That one threw everyone for a loop; especially my father. He's been preparing for death for 20 years and is so shocked it hasn't happened yet!

How did I feel? Scared. Sad. Lonely. Where's my friend? Who is this snappy, angry woman in the bed? Doesn't she know how hard this is on my sister and me? At the end of the day, after almost a week of waiting for a bed in a Phoenix hospital and innumerable tests, the doctors tell us she has a narrowed artery behind her left eye. It has been narrow since birth. Now, with age, it is more narrow and this is where the problem lies. There is nothing to be done and nothing to worry about. She will need to take some blood thinning medication and go home. Right. Don't worry, be happy!

My sister and I heave a sigh of relief and leave to make phone calls. We have lots of friends and relatives to call; it is exhausting to repeat the news so many times. Next time there is a crisis, we're going to have a phone tree! Then, in the middle of my calling, I start weeping.

The fear, the relief, the realization that my mother was here now and someday would truly be gone, all came crashing in on me at once. My dear mother, we have so much fun together, we drive each other crazy, we are the same in so many ways.

There are so many memories I treasure, I'd like to share some with you. As a child, I see myself sitting on her lap, with my brothers and sister all around, listening while she reads from *Winnie the Pooh* or *Treasure Island*. Then, in the kitchen, where all good things were created, I'm smelling the fragrance of good food and know the love that was put into it. One of my favorite things to do growing up was to help her get dressed for a night out with my father, while watching her transform from every day Mother to elegant Wife.

She was always a mother first. When I was in early labor with Morgan, she knew it would be many hours until the birth. She wanted to distract me and keep an eye on me both, so she insisted I drive the neighborhood with her, registering voters! It was certainly distracting. When my sister was having her second baby, she had a very difficult delivery. Because of modern attitudes and facilities, we could all be there in the room with her. My mother arrived late in the labor, anxious to be part of the birth. Janet especially wanted Mother there, but when Mother arrived, Janet was having such a difficult time, cries of pain emanated from the birthing room. I found my mother standing stock-still against the wall outside the room, eyes wide with terror, tears streaming down her face. I encouraged her to come in, but she couldn't. The nursing supervisor came by and offered to take her to a waiting area where she might be more comfortable. Still the cries came from the room and my mother, not able to go in, still could not leave her daughter in such pain and stood there, shaking, tears falling from her eyes. At the moment of Max's birth, I grabbed my mother, who upon seeing her grandson, still wet from birth, began weeping again, this time, with tears of joy. She claims she has faulty tear ducts.

So many proud moments I have thinking of her, she is a much loved and well-thought-of woman in our community. The word generous is always used when people speak of this kind and intelligent woman. As my grandma taught me, I always tell people to tell those closest to them how much they love them. Yet, have *I* told *her*? Will I tell her in time? When my mother reads this, I hope she has just an inkling of my joy, in having chosen her to be one of my most loving teachers.

FOUR

Spring
Always Comes

Cougar Tracks

Dear Waiki,

I know I've shared funny stories with you about the man that first introduced me to a life full of Spirit. Here is the story of our final time together.

February 19, 2001

It was one o'clock on a clear, crisp winter afternoon. The snow and mud still scrunched as the mud gave way to a softer ooze. Stately, naked cottonwoods stood sentry to the spring-fed creek, running cold through rounded, soft, sensual snow hugging its banks. The sounds of multiple thumps boomed through the forest, followed by the creaking of the pine boughs as they readjusted to their lighter load. Bird song rang out, as towhees, scrub jays, nuthatches and bushtits frantically foraged in the snow-filled forest.

I walked slowly, drinking all this in, moving as if in a cathedral; quietly, respectfully, with a sense of joy and awe. Tracks of rabbits, raccoons, deer, birds and bobcat crossed my path, as I made my way along my favorite trail. Many dog tracks were present, with their accompanying human companions' prints.

I came to the split in the trail, and here the snow had melted substantially since our whiteout on Valentine's Day. This particular aspect of the trail had received a lot of activity, both animal and human; the snow was stamped down to four inches or so in places. Many people elected to turn around at this point or skirt the stream, continuing on the trail to the right, staying on the more maintained, domesticated road. Standing at the trail split, scanning the snow for more tracks, I marveled at the life teeming in the forest that one rarely sees. After an easy decision, I turned to the left, to follow the trail I knew was present, but was not visible in the pristine snow. I ventured forth, plowing the snow that came to my knees. Pushing ahead, I was in heaven.

Walking became difficult as I made my way, guessing at times where the trail lay. I shed layers of clothing as my temperature and pulse rose with the exertion. Many deer tracks intersected my route. I imagined the deer, reclusive in nature, moving slowly, ears twitching, looking all around as they scrunched quietly and daintily through the snow. Puzzled as I made my way along the trail, I was following an animal I was sure was a bobcat. The prints seemed to shift and change with the terrain; as an amateur, I was easily confused. On my return home I laughed as I discovered that, indeed, I had been following the trail of a bobcat. He had been going down the trail I was going up; thus, my befuddlement.

Making my way back to where the trails joined, eyes scanning constantly for more animal tracks, I stopped, stunned. Right in front of me, amid the dog, human and squirrel prints, was the one track I always know when I see it: the mountain lion. Cougar, puma, mountain lion, these are all monikers for the largest and most elusive of our local forest beasts. A big one, too, from the width and depth of the paw marks. Using my palm as a guide, I measured the prints marching out of the forest. His paw was at least four inches from front to back and almost equal side to side. The indentations between the toes were picture perfect; the rounded characteristic feline print with no nail marks showing, was classic.

Fascinated, I followed the tracks, realizing they were headed out of the forest, the way I had walked in. How could I have missed them? They were so large and obvious. My curiosity was piqued and I simply followed, marveling at the size and beauty, imagining the magnificent creature they belonged to.

Close to the trail's end, the tracks turned left, toward the creek. They made a circle in the snow under a large juniper tree, headed in the direction of the stream and were gone. Searching the area, I couldn't pick up the trail. With something close to sadness, I turned to leave. It was now 2:15 and I was due at my aunt's.

I returned home after visiting and shopping, and my husband came to greet me and help with groceries. Bouncing to the music playing on the radio, I opened my car door, then realized something was very wrong with Al. Turning down the music, I heard him say,

"Mark had a massive cerebral hemorrhage." Mark Duke[39] was one of our dearest friends, an irreverent theater director and actor. They definitely broke the mold on this one, much to our constant delight and amazement. I came into stillness, having been worried for some time about my hard-living friend.

As I stared out the front window, I prepared to hear of his death. "Who found him?"

I was already wondering how I was going to live without his constant, accurate, wisecracking assessments, along with his teddy-bear softness that few knew. Mark and I had a unique relationship. Many thought it odd, as we appeared to be polar opposites. But in reality, it was very complementary. He opened my eyes to some of the grittier aspects of life, and my upbeat attitude allowed him to see others in a kinder, less negative light.

I then heard the pain in Al's voice, as it broke on the news that poured from his soul, "He had it during workshop . . . ."

"Oh, my God!" was all I could manage, as I jumped from the truck to hold my beloved as he shook and sobbed. Mark held an acting workshop every Sunday afternoon in his home; he had a strong following both new and old. Al composed himself to inform me that Mark had been airlifted to Phoenix and was not expected to live. Liz,[40] Mark's ex-wife and best friend, was already on her way.

With an intensity I have in times of crisis, I calmly gave orders, prepared an overnight bag and made phone calls. Al tried to tell me Mark had lost consciousness at his home and had never regained it, telling me, "He won't even know you're there." Stubbornly and emotionless, I could only reply, "He'll know." I couldn't cry, couldn't shake, could only focus on the moment at hand. If I broke now, I'd never make the drive to Phoenix. As I got ready to leave, I could feel the enormity of Al's grief. As I turned to him, the haunted look in his

39   Mark P. Duke: musician, actor, director. Graduate of The Estelle Harmon School of Acting, he was most proud of his Gong Show trophy. Mark and Liz Story together owned The Theatre, where Mark held acting workshops and staged plays. In addition, he produced a number of Liz Story's albums. His life was one large tragicomedy, and a footnote hardly does him justice.
40   Liz Story: concert pianist, Mark and Liz were married from 1984-1990. They moved to Prescott from Los Angeles in 1987.
       Internationally acclaimed touring artist, Liz is recognized as one of the most praised and popular members of the groundbreaking Windham Hill roster. A Steinway artist, Liz has been called "one of the most imaginative solo pianists." She has lectured on music and astrology and has been nominated for three Grammys. Liz has recorded nine CDs and has performed on many other artists' recordings. Biography courtesy of: www.worldpuja.org/EVENTS/ARCHIVES/FORUM/lizbio.htm
       Through Mark's acting workshop I met Liz, and the gift of our relationship pulled us through many dark moments following Mark's death. It was a beautiful thing he did, bringing us together; only he knew the myriad ways we would both benefit.

eyes revealed a man who had lost his best friend. He had been there with Mark; he was not prepared to see any more. As the tears spilled down his cheeks, he could only whisper quietly, "I—can't—go. Is that okay?" As we removed his items from my overnight bag, I reassured him as best I could. As much as I wanted to stay and console him, Al was alive, while my dear friend lay near death.

As I stood pumping gas for my trip south, a distinct voice said to me, "Pay attention. See the day—record the moment." All street activity and other surrounding movements grew crystal clear in detail. Late afternoon sun dipping behind the horizon, the air was taking on its winter chill. Snow lay sprinkled on the face of Thumb Butte, our city's natural landmark. There was not a cloud in our southwest sky. A laughing couple made their way up a steep incline adjacent to the little gas station while cars passed quietly on the main street of town. It seemed a surreal, small-town scene, set in winter on a day everyone cherished.

"Yes, Mark, I'll remember this moment. I'm sending it to you right now, see the sun as it goes down? All this, I'm sending your way . . . ." The moment dissolved as quickly as it appeared. I made a detour to pick up Joanne, another friend and acting companion of Mark's, and we were on our way. It was a bizarre, two-hour drive, discussing the unbelievability of death, old stories, some jokes and as few tears as I could get away with.

We arrived at Barrow Neurological Institute to find Liz in chaos and medical personnel asking her if they could unhook Mark from life support for a test of some kind. She was distraught beyond belief, yet deeply moved by the fact we had come.

"What else could we do?" I inquired, adding other silly yet reassuring things, along the line that people say when they are unable to address the horror in front of them. Now she would not have to make decisions on her own; although legally she was the person to speak for Mark, she very much wanted this to be a group process.

We now turned our attention to Mark. Lying in the hospital bed, life support systems whirring and pulsing, he didn't look too bad. Darn good, actually. I had prepared Joanne, saying he would probably look pale and lifeless. The wonders of modern medicine gave the impression of a deep, peaceful sleep for someone who now couldn't possibly tie his own shoelaces. Even his hair, about which he was always so particular, was not a bit out of place. There is a peculiarity in our culture that leads us to focus on strange things when confronted with death and dying. In my case, the necessity of bringing a brush with me to comb Mark's hair, knowing it had been important to him once, so it was important to me now. We could almost believe he was fine except that he never sat up and cracked jokes, remarking how lamentably we all were behaving. He joked about everything, audacious mostly; he loved to shock me especially. I suppose deep down inside he knew that I liked being shocked; then I could act outraged that he'd say such a thing. High drama. We were a good team.

In the short hours we shared with our friend, we alternately laughed, cried, held each other and simply walked away when it became too much to bear. Our good friend Milton joined us, as we formed a square of Love around Mark. Mark may no longer have been with us embodied in his physical form, but he certainly was there in a much stronger, vibrant way that only Spirit can be. It was as if he formed the fifth point of a pentagon above the bed, in his last moments connected to life support.

After discussing Mark's apparent incompatibility with life, the nurse gently asked if he would have wanted to be an organ donor. Immediately, in a vision, I saw his eyes, continuing on to assist others. I lovingly quipped, "Yeah! I just wouldn't take his lungs or his liver!" It was delightful to be able to laugh in such a moment. He drank quite a bit and never would quit smoking. I think he just liked his vices too much to give them up. Before we could set him eternally free, however, we had to answer forty-plus questions for the organ nurse so the foundation could use his eyes and tissues.

The questions began with "Has your friend been diagnosed with HIV or AIDS that you know of? Has your friend had unprotected sex in the last six months with another man that you know of?" "No—I don't think so . . . ." A bit unsure how to proceed, we all looked at Milton. "Not with me!" was his appropriate, hilarious-in-the-moment, response. The bizarre and obscure disease list continued, along with questions about drug use and other things that would make him an unlikely candidate for donation. Somewhere around twenty questions I commented that "Mark's getting healthier all the time!" Humor is a great defense mechanism, especially when dealing with someone whose life had so much tragedy, a life such as Mark's. That was why he sought comedy in life; he used to say that it was in tragedy that comedy was found. Strange, given all those nasty diseases Mark didn't have, just the same, he was by all rights dead.

That task completed, we all stood guard while the nurses gently and reverently removed the machines and tubing. Talking to him all the while, they treated him like a tender infant. With their leaving, we took up our places once again for a final farewell. My statue of Athena sat on Mark's right shoulder, an angel he gave me sat on his left, while my head lay on the pillow, next to his. Liz lay on the bed, holding his left hand, crooning to him in between sobs. Joanne sat at his feet, mute with shock and grief. Milton sat in a chair, holding his right hand, telling Mark to "Go to the Light, Mark, go to the Light." Weeping, I was reluctant to give up my wild friend who had taught me so much.

The voice I had heard earlier in the evening spoke again, but this time with the gravelly, cigarette-charred resonance that was so clearly Mark's.

"C'mon, you guys! It's beginning to look a little maudlin around here . . . ." Looking up at his face, his color had begun to fade to a definite, unhealthy green. He didn't look so good, not any more.

"C'mon, you guys," I mimicked, "he's needing makeup, time to go." I removed my weavings and sacred statues, and packed it in. I went back for one last kiss and hug goodbye and attempted to cover his face. Unable to do so, we left.

Only many hours later, nearing five in the morning, as I finally drifted toward sleep, did I remember the mountain lion's tracks. It was the previous afternoon that I had followed in the cougar's footsteps. He had turned as if to say goodbye, and was gone. It was the exact time that my caustic, spiritually connected friend truly passed from this earth. Mark knew I would know it was his Spirit, and above all, appreciate the drama.

Goodbye, my love, my friend, my teacher and best cheerleader. Lord, how I will miss you.

Maybe I Haven't Forgotten?

Surrounded by death of late, it crosses my mind a lot. Driving to see my friend Eddie, who was dying of AIDS, I had two hot fudge sundaes that he had requested. Waiting at a stoplight, I thought of my dear friend, Mark, who died two months ago in late February. Liz, his ex-wife, said she felt that he had to go so he could come back right away. I have heard talk in the spiritual community of just that sort of thing—that we will remember all we've learned when we return and will be moving at a much faster speed in regard to spiritual growth and transformation. This all rocketed through my awareness, as thoughts often do, and I said out loud, "When I die, I want to come right back—if that's appropriate, or okay to ask—I want to come right back! And I want to remember everything! Not start over, remember it all!" A voice that seemed to come on the breeze over my left shoulder, wafted in front of me and stated, "And why do you think you've forgotten anything? What makes you think you've forgotten, that you don't know all you knew?"

My car crept around the corner as the light changed to green, while I contemplated the questions put before me.

Eddie's Gift

Thank you, my blessed teacher. I came to assist you. In the end, of course, it was I who was assisted. You were dying. I came with the hope of easing your pain. We joined Spirit together, and man, what a ride! Our spirits joined and you showed me the eagles with which you flew, the places you knew existed, the realities where you knew you would go.

I thank you.

You shared your honesty. You taught me to withhold judgment. The determination you showed, even in those last days, makes me get up and go, no matter how I may feel in the morning. My slight little problems seem just that.

I thank you.

You received my ministrations, my Love, my Gift of Spirit, without so much as a blink of an eye.

I thank you.

Above all, because of your acceptance of my work, your faith in me as a healing assistant, you gave me the confidence to remove the final mask of who I am and the Gift of Spirit I have to offer humanity.

I really, really thank you.

Shattered Glass

Somehow I got through it all.
The wake, the arrangements, the cremation and the party.
No memorial or service for this man; only a party would do.
A party to reconnect, to tell stories, to drink excessively and say special
    goodbyes.
Did he know how many cared? Did he know how many he touched?
The mourners gone, I am left alone with my grief and solitude.
Time passes, life seems amazingly difficult and the oddest little things
    bring me to tears and rage.
The rage takes longer.
I thought I'd get out of the grief process without that one. It, too,
    comes and goes.

Three months pass. The weekends are especially difficult; Mark died
    on a Sunday.
Saturday, at an art exhibit, there is the most enormous statue of
    Harvey[41] I've ever seen. Thoughts of theater and characters, late
    nights and love pass swiftly as I stare in wonderment at the rabbit.
The glass begins to shatter; there are people everywhere. Quickly I
    leave, the glass of my containment falling away, bit by bit, leaving
    shards behind me as I run. Alone at last, not wanting to be stared
    at, I collapse and sob. The thick rainbow prisms glisten in the sun.

The wind blows, it sets me on edge. My beloved is abrupt; the glass
    again begins to crack.
So many everyday occurrences jar me—the grocery store, Mark's truck
    in the parking lot.
Shock, confusion, disbelief, "Where is he?" begins to form when I realize

---

41   Harvey: a pooka, an invisible rabbit, from the play by the same name. Mark Duke directed
    Harvey at Prescott Fine Arts Association, 1989.

Mark's friend, Sean, is in the truck. The cracks are getting longer and more plentiful.

I attempt to cook, to provide love for my family, the glass is getting unstable.
"Got to go to the store, just a couple of things . . . " somehow seems so important.
Laughing young clerks: "She really cracks me up," the young lady comments. The glass lies at my feet as I pay my bill. Tears streaming down my face, "Yes," I reply, "keep up the laughter."

Mark's comedy and jokes ring in my ears. Did he know how much I laughed?
Yes, he knew and the glass was shattered; to be restored for another day.

Life Takes a Left Turn

My Dearest Waiki,

I came across a story I wrote almost ten years ago, when this whole Divine Madness began. I found one aspect of my time in the hospital particularly funny, considering my reality now. I was hearing voices and was worried if I mentioned anything to the nurses or doctors they would lock me up. Not only do I hear voices these days and admit it (actually, it's only One voice), but I follow and trust in what it tells me. The irony of it all! I'll just give you the story and you'll understand how my life was changed forever.

July 1992

The brick wall is red, about 20 feet out my window as I open my eyes. There is nothing else. No sky, no other buildings, just the red brick wall. Then voices—my eyes search as I attempt to move my head and take in the bizarre surroundings. One of the voices belongs to my father and he comments, "It's okay honey, you're in the ICU (Intensive Care Unit)." No, that is certainly not okay with me, and how . . . I drift away. More voices, faces unrecognizable. The smiling doctor says, "Well, we don't know what you do have, but we know you don't have AIDS or syphilis!" Great. That is my biggest concern— is that supposed to inspire confidence? It's all so foggy, I try to stay awake, sleep takes me.

The room is dark now; it must be night. Things are unclear, confusing. Not to be indelicate, but there seems to be something very large and uncomfortable stuffed between my thighs, tracing further up into my body. I tug and pull but it won't budge, then someone says, "No! Don't do that!" I'm confused, we struggle and I shout "I want it out!" "Stop!" she says, "It's a catheter; do you think you can urinate on your own?" "Of course!" God, who do they think I am? Can I urinate by myself? Have they taken leave of their senses? Abruptly, I drift back into unconsciousness.

Morning. Bustling, friendly people. "Come to take blood from your arm," someone says. Sure, why not? My head is starting to throb and many questions are beginning to form. Now, I need to urinate and somehow I summon help. "We'll use the bedpan since you don't have your catheter now; can you roll over?" "Of course!" I reply. What is with these people? I attempt to turn to my right side—AAARGH!! Every muscle in my body screams in torment. What is wrong with me? My head hurts, every single muscle is in agony, I slip into welcome darkness as soon as the task is completed.

More doctors now with their clipboards huddle around my bed. There is a battery of questions, tests, pokes, turns of the head. "What day is it?" "Who gives a damn?" I think. "What year is it, who is President?" they inquire. "1973!" hmm . . . that doesn't seem quite right. "What's your name?" I do know that. Marilyn Gilliland. "No, no, no." All wrong. I weep, they leave shaking their heads.

One of the kind nurses informs me it is August 17, 1991. My name is Marilyn Markham; I am divorced and have taken my family name back. I am in Yavapai Regional Medical Center, in their Intensive Care Unit. George Bush is President. Really, not Ronald Reagan. This is all way too much to absorb. My head is pounding to match my fast pulse rate, they won't give me anything for the pain, and I just want to go to sleep.

A bit of order begins to come into my world now that I know where I am. The lab people come by regularly to take blood. The nurses take vital signs constantly it seems and play what I refer to as "the question game." I'm getting better at it, and remember the proper answers most of the time. No one gives me answers, though. Why am I here? "We don't know what you have, yet." "Well, what do they think I have?" I inquire. The nurses just look uncomfortable and say they "just don't know."

Upon awakening from another bit of sleep, there is someone most dear to me whom I *do* recognize, and it is my mother. I am overwhelmed by seeing a familiar face, and I can't wait to feel her wonderful hug. But, wait, what is this? She is putting on a mask and gown! Many realizations come flooding back. I am a registered nurse and we use masks and gowns for patients who either have extremely infectious diseases or whose immune systems are compromised.

"Why?" I ask. "They're just being cautious," she assures me. But cautious for whom, I wonder, my mother or me?

More people come in and out. Attempts to move still cause my muscles to shriek in pain and I wonder how they got this way. Many other questions continue to go unanswered. Oh, look, there's a sweet little boy coming in with a woman who looks vaguely familiar. "Oh my God!" I shout to myself as she speaks the boy's name. "Morgan wanted to come see you." He rushes to me and we hold each other tight. This is my son; how could I have forgotten my only son? They leave too soon and I am on an emotional roller coaster of tears, headache, muscle aches and the awareness that there is a very empty place in my head where there used to be knowledge and *I want it back!*

Another day dawns; there is a goal to be accomplished. I must get to the toilet across the room by myself. It's really not too very far, can't be more than six feet from the bed, and I'm young! How young? Thirty four, so they tell me, and who are they to lie? My awkward attempts to roll over and sit up attracts one of the nurses, so we discuss how to go about this. I now take in all I'm hooked to. Two intravenous (IV) bottles, a heart monitor and the ever-present floppy gown. One less accouterment since I lost the catheter, but a heart monitor? They must do that to everyone here since it's an ICU, I rationalize, because by now I have remembered that I work downstairs on the medical-surgical floor and am versed in such things; I take care of people, not the other way around. Well, on to the problem at hand. The nurse helps me sit up, then I feel an odd combination of being so dizzy and about to faint, and feeling like one of those detectives in all those mystery stories I read where the heroine gets hit over the head. The room does literally swim, just as in the books, but then things come into focus after I sit there a few minutes. "Okay to stand?" the nurse asks. "Sure," I respond with Olympic determination. I stand! Sweating, it's now or never. The toilet is my goal as I stay focused, feeling my muscles bellow for mercy as if I had just run a triathlon with no conditioning. Finally we arrive, none too soon, as I collapse, covered with sweat. The doctors tell me I'm running a fever with a high white count; surely that's where all the sweat is coming from. Nothing to do with the fact that it was the hardest walk I ever made in my life, my urine is brick red like the wall outside, my head is beating like a drum and I still have to walk back. Somehow I make it back and drop off into a glorious sleep.

The night shift comes on and we play the question game while taking vital signs—blood pressure, pulse, temperature and respirations. I get all the answers right except I don't quite understand the concept of advancing a day, so I get the date wrong. Damn. Some memory has been returning and I remember how to fix the IV machine when it is beeping, telling my sister-in-law in a slurry voice, "Don't worry, I'm a nurse!" She doesn't look convinced. At times I recognize individuals who come to see me, but more important to me, I can walk, albeit shakily and with a lot of sweating, to the toilet and back by myself! Triumph at last!

Another day in the ICU and finally there are some answers to my questions. "Good morning, I'm Dr. Smith, the neurologist who your doctor, Dr. Inscore called in on consultation." This is really how doctors talk, I know, because I'm a nurse and on familiar ground here. "You're a very sick woman and we're not exactly sure what you have, but we think you have viral encephalitis." What's that, I wonder, never heard of it, must write it down. He then proceeds to give me all the particulars of all the lab work they'd been doing: 35,000 white blood count (wbc) (7-10,000 is normal), wbc in spinal fluid (none is normal). "Spinal fluid?" I question, "How . . . ?" "Spinal tap, you were in a coma," he responds.

A coma—thoughts of every coma case I ever heard of raced through my brain. "How bad? How many days?" The doctor answers "Two days. And you had seizures, quite a few seizures. We don't know exactly how many because you were already in a coma when you were found, and having seizures at the time." "Seizures?" I inquire, this is all too much to take. "Yes, grand mal, *status epilepticus*." Oh, sweet Jesus, "Status?" All my nursing knowledge of this condition responds quickly and I know exactly what he is talking about. Status epilepticus is when you have grand mal seizures (convulsions) one after another without a break. It can fry your brain, depriving it of oxygen because you don't breathe during status if they don't get it stopped. It can kill you.

He continues. "There is a blood test we do that tests muscle activity, giving us an idea how many seizures you might have had before you were found. The test showed five to ten times the normal, so we think you may have had anywhere from ten to twenty seizures before you were brought to the hospital. You may have noticed some muscle soreness."

"Yes," I had noticed. "Where do we go from here?" I asked.

"We'll keep you under observation for a while, continue giving you IV antibiotics and see from there."

"When do I get to go home?" Wait and see, I'm told. "When can I eat?" "Oh, you're hungry?" Boy, is this what it's like being on this side of the bed? "Yes, I'm hungry! Enough to eat a regular meal!"

"Well, we better start with clear liquids and advance to a regular diet in a few days after we see how you do."

Damn it, they're going to treat me just like a regular patient and I want to eat! "Can I have something for my headache?"

"No, we gave you quite a bit of morphine and Valium for the seizures, and now well, we need to see how you'll do without all that on board."

Wonder what that was all about? It was the only time in our conversation he seemed a bit awkward. I was to find out later they needed to see me without any narcotics to determine if I had lost mental function, a somewhat rare occurrence with encephalitis, but it does happen. In addition, with all the seizures, that can amount to a loss of brain cells. This was a lot to take in all at once. I drifted back to my fitful sleep after the good doctor left.

Fitful it was. Many people came in and out during the day, some familiar and some not. I received my first bed bath, not able to sit up long enough to do it myself. Had I not been so confused, I'm sure there would have been inspirational thoughts about being a helpless nurse and all the lessons I would learn. But not on this day; that would come much later. Some days, as I lay in my hospital bed, I heard voices. My memory is fuzzy as to what was actually said, but my impression was a lot of nonsense, but with a sure sense what was happening to me wasn't normal. When my brother, a physician, came to visit, I quietly inquired about the voices. "Could I be having auditory (hearing) hallucinations?" I was too frightened to ask anyone else about my voices. "They" might put me in a stranger place yet, if I started spouting off about voices in my head.

"Yes," he assured me, "anything that might be affected by the nervous system is game." Well! That covers some ground! A sense of relief washed over me just the same; I wasn't going crazy in addition to everything else.

In the first week after my coma, I had difficulty remembering things that had happened in the previous five to ten years. My son was nine at the time; thus my memory failed initially regarding his existence. In addition, my memory failed in regard to my employment, my divorce, friends who had married, and friends who had died. In the weeks and months that followed I would get most of my memory back, but some is simply gone forever. My emotional state was a mess. The tears flowed like the Colorado; I was frustrated with my head and willing my body to do things it simply refused to do. I wanted my life back, and it didn't look like that was going to happen any time in the near future.

After a week in the ICU, I was moved down to the medical-surgical floor where I had been working just the week before—in a hospital bed, unable to sit up for the short ride from one floor to the next. Still, this was a big move, and I was looking forward to another big goal: being able to sit long enough to shower and have my hair washed. Six days my hair had gone unwashed; just shows you how vanity can go down the drain in such circumstances.

Life then became a series of goals, one to the next. Walking 20 feet down the hallway and back, sitting up in an armchair while my bed was made, helping now with the bath and hair routine. It all came painfully slow to my liking. Having always been a woman of speed—hurry, hurry, have to experience everything. Now life slowed to the most basic elements. Looking back, I didn't think of these tasks as goals, I just knew I had to accomplish them. I walked that long hall to the nurses station for pain medicine when I really just wanted to use the buzzer, knowing that to get better, I had to. All my training and upbringing put me on auto-pilot. That was useful then, but later became an obstacle.

Ten days after awakening from my coma, I left the hospital for my parents' home, thinking to be there only a few days, thinking them silly for renting a hospital bed for me. The true measure of my illness and lack of judgment still had not sunk in. Or had I not let it? Three weeks later, I finally returned to my own home. I had been gone a month and a lifetime.

The memory loss was still a problem, frightening, frustrating and later, embarrassing. The three years before my illness still had some large black holes. My mind didn't save new memories so well, either. I developed great compassion for the aging and senile. At times a memory could be coaxed back with information from another person. The times that remained hidden were dark moments, indeed. Old schoolmates just couldn't seem to understand how I could not know who they were—fortunately, coworkers knew what had happened to me and gave me quick relief by telling me their names. The best memories, though, were the ones I remembered on my own. Someone would walk into my room and I would exclaim, "You're so and so! I know who you are!" That always made me feel I might beat this thing after all.

The rest of my acute recovery was spent walking farther, doing simple chores and letting my body recover with lots of rest. The other problem besides the memory difficulties was fatigue. I simply didn't have any "get up and go," and little in the way of energy reserves. This was an area of encephalitis I knew nothing about—the long-term effects of this unusual illness that can be so difficult to adjust to. But adjust I must, so naps every day are how I accomplish that.

Viral meningoencephalitis was the actual diagnosis of my illness, with unknown cause. Encephalitis, loosely defined, is an inflammation of the brain and its coverings, producing headache, fever, drowsiness, delirium, coma and, rarely, death (*Dorland's Illustrated Medical Dictionary*). There are many causes, although primarily it is seen in epidemic form caused by the bite of a tick or mosquito or secondary to another infection. All the nursing and medical books will tell you that relief of symptoms is paramount and prevention of further complications is imperative. What they don't tell you is that the disease can have debilitating effects depending on the severity of the illness, and the recovery time is generally three to five years or, in some cases, longer. Every case, of course, is individual, so each recovery is also different. It is not like measles or the flu that have pretty standard phases of the disease, and that is precisely what can be so frustrating. The recovery period depends on how the patient "presents." Since I presented in a coma with multiple seizures, my recovery could be longer and more unpredictable, as opposed to someone who presents less severely. The memory problems seem to get better with time, and the younger the patient the better the recovery.

Any illness that puts an adult out of work for an extended period of time can put great strain on the individual, the family and the people they have contact with. It can lead to difficulty in defining ourselves when our life, livelihood and money-making ability are taken from us. Our society defines us and stereotypes us by what we do for a living more than by who we are. When was the last time you met someone new and had a conversation, without asking what they did for a living? Or saw someone you haven't seen in a long time, and of course you want to know what they're doing—still at the same job? Trying something different? My therapist refers to people like me as the "walking wounded." We look all right, sound fine, just can't hold a job. And, as a single mother, that can be very discouraging. It requires you to look very deep inside to find someone you really like all by yourself, without the benefit of a regular nine-to-five job to define you. I happen to have lots of abilities, because I was switching careers at the time I got ill, and have done a number of things on the side to make ends meet. So I just choose what I want to be that day, a graphic designer, writer, nurse, baker or just plain me when asked that all important question "So, what are you doing these days?" Sometimes I just answer "Oh, a little of this, a little of that," but that can really throw some people, so I don't use it much.

Encephalitis can be similar to a head injury in the confusion, frustration and denial it can cause, but it is also unique and any difficulties need to be taken one day at a time. This is, of course, the lesson many people will tell you who have had encephalitis or any other life-threatening illness—that it is essential to take one day at a time. It's difficult to go through something like that without truly getting the message to slow down and smell the roses. The hope, of course, is that our fellow humans can learn some of the lessons along with us.

Waiki, as I sit and contemplate that time so long ago, and what I learned, the above lesson shouts for attention. Our fast-paced world seems to move faster and faster, and we struggle to catch up. We can't catch up, nor should we try. We need to still our bodies and minds, and begin anew, walking with a different, more graceful step.

The Voice of Grace

Dearest Waiki,

As I finished transcribing the story, Life Takes a Left Turn, *I considered the voice I now hear and respond to so regularly. I pondered when I knew it was a voice of Higher Power, and therefore a voice to listen to. Then I remembered the morning I heard it.*

While sitting in my backyard one sunny, early spring day in 1994, I contemplated a difficult problem. My former husband and I shared joint custody of our son, Morgan. Along with some other issues, we had been having difficulties with scheduling weekends, as I tended to be more spontaneous and Morgan's father preferred to stick to a schedule. We had gone back to see a therapist we had once seen together, to determine if we could resolve our predicament. The sessions seemed to be going nowhere and I felt the counselor was being one-sided, not a mediator at all. I called him at home one evening to discuss my viewpoint, only to discover my assessment was correct. The therapist said it was a power issue, and he felt he needed to side with my ex-husband. Wanting to get on with the process, I was determined to solve the problem myself and come to an agreeable solution.

Sitting in my grandmother's old wrought iron chair with my eyes closed, the question I asked was this: "If I give over power to Morgan's father, what do I gain?" Quite literally and unexpectedly, a bright golden light shone upon me and a powerful voice said, "You gain Grace." Wow! Grace it is! With a complete shift in my attitude toward the situation and my ex-husband, I rose from the chair and knew that I would do whatever it took to make the situation amenable to him. I would make it as comfortable and stress-free as possible for my son, and, by doing so, I would gain something I wasn't so sure about, but I knew would impact my life in a vast way.

In the end, it did turn into a win-win situation for all. Morgan and his father both felt secure with a definite schedule. I learned to put another's needs ahead of mine, someone with whom I'd been in love with once, but couldn't live with any longer, due to vast differences. Maybe it was Grace I gained. Whatever it was, it is still somewhat indescribable, but it sure does feel good. And I have learned to listen to the voice that suggested it.

What Is Love?

Musings from a Sunday evening. Defining again . . . sure don't like the way it limits. In the end, I just want people to say of me that I moved Love. This is my Path, my intent, with no attachment to the form in which it will be given to the world. This has been difficult, not knowing the form my intent will take, but recognizing the necessity of letting go.

Every day I am challenged to not define, "What do you do?" "What do you call yourself?" Preparing for a psychic fair recently, I refuse a title. I fit into all the categories. I simply Love. I provide myself as a conduit for Spirit to flow through for the best outcome of the individual. Call it what you will, but don't label me. Why would you want to label, thus limiting Love?

What is Love? Why would anyone want to be Love?
Love encourages healing and kindness and it makes us smile.
It encourages the body to feel better in a special, soothing, comforting way.
This is just a bit of what Love does.

Love reaches out in the middle of the night, to soothe the brow, to "walk the beat."
Love delights in the clink of glasses, the gay voices coupled with the clanging piano playing of yesteryear.

Love understands and mourns the children in the gutter, their lack of shelter, and occasionally is successful in easing the burden they've chosen in life.
Love holds the greasy wino while wiping the spittle from his chin.
Love exclaims with the voices of the lovers, pulled to each other with their primal need.

It sighs with them in their nest of completion.
Love loves.

Love sees everything as the same: wonderful, horrible and perfect in
everything we do, we see, and everything we can possibly imagine.
Loves sees this all, feels it, experiences it, understands it, revels in it, is
repulsed by it and knows it will go on always, even as it pulls us
toward the One.
Love simply Loves it all.

Love Is All!

Rituals of Healing

Dearest Américo,

I guess you could say I've been a healer all my life. In addition, I've been an observer of miracles. At the age of five, wearing my nurse's cap and cape, I cared for various dolls, people or animals. God, I loved that cape! Blue on the outside, red on the inside, with a gold clasp at the neck. Over the left breast was a medical insignia, printed in gold. There was never a doubt I would be a nurse. I would be the Florence Nightingale of the 20th century, save the world and that was that. Never was there a question in my mind.

Once, when my brother Richard was a teenager, he injured himself, putting a considerable gash in the side of his head, requiring many stitches. He came home from the hospital with a large bandage encircling his skull, walking like a man who has had too much to drink. Forcing him onto the couch in the sun room, I quickly took charge, and began to minister to him. I slept by his bed, catering to his needs, making sure he recovered straightaway. I was 11. True to my style of knowing what's best for others, I never asked Richard how he felt about my care, just took charge, and he recovered nicely. Now, however, I have learned to ask if people want my assistance.

As you know, I did go on to be a nurse, but it wasn't until I connected with you, Américo, that my success assisting others to heal on a wholly different plane really began. It was during the two weeks I spent with you in Utah that I learned to unlearn, to connect with the Cosmos, to perceive energy and shift it. These are just a few things you shared.

When I returned home from Utah, I had a brief visit with my friend Dick. With much enthusiasm, I explained what I had been learning. Dick saw something in me I couldn't at the time, and it was he who sent me my first client. Terry Richardson (not his real name), had torn his bicep muscle when he lost his footing exiting his truck. When his foot slipped, he reached for the support above the window, thus focusing all his weight on his right arm. *According to an orthopedic surgeon, it was a "catastrophic injury." The surgeon suggested that the only way to repair it was to operate. Terry decided he wanted to try an alternative method, so Dick gave him my telephone number and we began to work together.*

When you look at a healthy bicep muscle, the muscle domes nicely out from the inner elbow, as it reaches toward the shoulder. Terry's right bicep, however, was flat. You could see where the muscle was holding on at the insertion points of the elbow; it looked as if a small string held it in place on each side. Every other day we worked for two hours. I let Spirit guide me as you had taught, utilizing stones when needed or energy when it was called for. Some days were like watching an operation; I realized we had to suture energetically from the inside out, working in layers, just as a surgeon would when sewing up a deep incision. There were times you and Pasqualito came to assist me. In my vision, I saw you wrap your tan and red scarf around all three of us as we stood over Terry, connecting us all, reassuring me I was not doing this alone. I would always have help. First from you, then the waikis of the mountains, and then assistance from all of the Universe. Besides, "I" wasn't "doing" anything. I was simply providing myself as a conduit for Spirit to flow through and allowing myself to be guided by Love.

I realize now it is a co-creation, a co-healing if you will, as I work with others to create a positive result. I don't really heal anybody, certainly not without their help. Two weeks from our introduction, with pride and excitement in his eyes, Terry rode his Harley-Davidson motorcycle down my driveway and turned around in my backyard. As you can well imagine, this was not something he had been able to do since his injury. He was just regaining his strength and the muscle had returned to a healthy looking, normal bicep. We worked together that last day and he left for Colorado to continue with therapy and rehabilitation. It was a great beginning for me, and the true joy of being filled with the Love of the Cosmos for the assistance of others was just starting to sink in.

You told us in your teachings that to heal someone you don't have to be physically present. After I returned home from the retreats, I learned to play with the energy, to ride the wind to be with you and the group still up north, and learned the infinite textures and nuances of this amazing force. As the summer wore on and turned to fall, my friend's daughter, Tiffany, just six years old and starting school in another state, was having abdominal difficulties. Tiffany and I had grown close in our short friendship; it dismayed me to think of her so ill. Her father, George, thought she might have eaten something peculiar on a trip to the Bahamas in late June. But she alternated between diarrhea and constipation for months, and now, starting school, was forced to wear a diaper to prevent accidents. This sweet, darling, somewhat shy girl having to wear a diaper to school; we can only imagine her mortification. The doctors said it was a "lazy colon" and were considering surgery because none of the other medical solutions had helped. I asked George if I could help. My assistance certainly couldn't hurt, so we set up a special time of day for us to work together. Tiffany rested while George read to her; meanwhile, I meditated two states away. Sitting in my meditation room, I worked with various energies and visuals, the most curious being my two new helpers.

The new helpers were two serpents. The snakes had made their presence known a month or so before. Working energetically on a friend with tendonitis, I had a vision of two snakes sitting on my head. In unison, they slithered down my arms as I watched in fascination. They gathered at my friend's inflamed elbow and sank their fangs into it. The opposite of venomous snakes, they sucked the inflammation out! Her elbow improved and she returned to her tennis game.

With Tiffany, they behaved differently. I saw her lying on her bed, eyes closed, and very relaxed. On her belly, curled up together sleeping, were my two snakes. They weren't there every day we worked together, apparently just when needed. After five days in healing meditation, approximately one-half hour to an hour each day, George called in anxious excitement. "Turn it off! She couldn't go before and now it's like a faucet! Turn it off!" I could hear the excitement and joy in his voice; Tiffany would have no need for surgery after all. With lots of whoops and hollers, we all congratulated ourselves and thanked the Cosmos. My dear little friend was recovering and did not have to take pills, enemas or endure the humiliation of wearing a diaper long after an appropriate age.

You may wonder why I tell you about such healings; you have said cancers can be cured with energy and Love, so this is not news to you. I am telling you because these experiences are so exciting for me. In addition, with intent and Love, anyone can do this work. I so want people to know that miracles happen every day, big and small. We just need to accept the beauty of this and know what to look for.

Intent and Love, that's all that's called for.

The Two Rules of the Universe

As nearly as I can tell, the Universe, the Cosmos, God and Goddess and everything in between, are relatively simple. *We* are simply incredibly adept at making it all very complicated. I feel there are really only two rules necessary for navigating in this enormously large and, paradoxically, infinitesimally small universe of ours. There are probably even fewer rules; it is entirely possible there are none, but for my brain, this seems easy to grasp. I didn't say it was easy to do, just easy to grasp.

The Two Rules, using my terminology, are open to interpretation. Number One: The only constant is change. Number Two: Ya gotta ask.

Number One, the only constant is change, means nothing stays the same, everything changes from one moment to the next. The very thought that just created this has shifted, another example has sprung to mind just in the writing of it; therefore, it has already changed. In times of crisis and stress we wish that life could just go back to how it was. Or we want to have the same body we had at twenty, or thirty or even six months ago. But none of these things are possible. Even if we do exercise and get into shape, we will never be the same—and how wonderful!

We have a strong tendency in this culture to romanticize the way it never was, to see things through rose-colored glasses. The greatest gift we can give ourselves is the ability to live in the moment. Enjoy drinking cold lemonade, watching the light glisten off the pine needles at just that particular time of day or indulge yourself in folding the laundry.

Watch young children play. Children are totally absorbed in what they are doing and have no interest in what might come later. I emphasize *might*, because the rest of us tend to live in the world of "what if" and "might" entirely too much. As we get caught up in either trying to live in the past or recapture it, as we attempt to control and then worry about the future, we fail to see the minute, glorious moments right in front of us. This is what people mean when they tell you to "live in the moment"—enjoy it! Focus on it, live it, be there! Of course there are times when we must plan things, think about the future or contemplate the past. Having said that, we can deliberate on these things while noticing what is going on around us at any given moment. As long as we get in the habit of being present as much as possible, we will live more in the moment and will be more adaptable when life inevitably does change.

Rule Number Two is a personal quote. "Ya gotta ask" means the Universe doesn't know what you want unless you state specifically. There are variations on the theme, such as "Energy flows where attention goes" and "Be careful what you ask for, you just might get it," to name just two. The latter I state as "Be careful what you ask for, you *always* get it. It just might not look exactly like what you had in mind." This has to do with the Law of Attraction. When we put our attention, energy or thoughts on a particular object, be it our health, our finances, our love life or whatever, that is what we attract; hence the Law of Attraction. What we have to remember is how we focus that energy. If we moan over the fact that we never get the raise that other employees get, we never have enough money or time to do the things we want, this is what we will continue to get. Although we are not literally asking the Universe for the aforementioned difficulties, we are, by virtue of our attention to it in this manner.

This is tricky territory here, so I'll give an example of my own. I had a history of dysfunctional relationships, typically involving men who were emotionally unavailable and less than honest. One day I heard myself say, "I just want somebody honest! I have such a thing about honesty, and I never seem to get someone truthful!" Bingo! I had inadvertently put my attention more on the fact I attracted less-than-honest men in my life and that's exactly what I got! I have wondered if all the cancers we see are due to better detection methods or due to the fact that we focus more on the cancer than on the health of the body.

It is essential with the Universe to be as specific as possible. Writing down what you want in a defined but open manner, can have tremendous power. I have a wonderful husband to prove it! A bit of advice here. When you're asking the Universe for things, be clean, clear, and let the Universe do its own work for your highest good. If you ask for financial security, don't put a price tag on it. Open to the myriad possibilities of being financially secure, whether it is writing a book, winning the lottery or being a consultant for your chosen field. There are many ways to be secure without necessarily earning an hour's pay for an hour's labor. Let the Universe do its work, be open to *all* the possibilities. In the end, it may be an hour's pay for an hour's work, but if it's doing something you absolutely love, that provides a roof over your head and a sense of satisfaction at the end of the day, is that not security?

So be flexible, knowing that life will change with or without your cooperation and be especially careful where and how you put your energy and focus in the world. Your life depends on it.

Mama Cocha Endures

September 18, 2001

Shattered glass, burning buildings, jet liners flying into the World Trade Center? The Pentagon? The buildings collapse, how many have died?

What is this madness? No one saw it coming, although the energy of the previous months had been tense for many.

What do we learn? What do we take away from this experience? Is there more to learn? Undoubtedly.

Words do not speak to the difficulty of comprehension. This is our global community. The television, our link to the immediate events. The horror occurs, it is broadcast instantaneously, then continuously for days after.

Still, we cannot grasp what has been done to us, how we have been attacked and assaulted. The reactions and responses are as varied as we are as a nation: fear, shock, disbelief. Where is my family?

I cannot imagine the trauma in the survivors' lives as they watch the planes fly headlong into the buildings, over and over again.

Then the anger begins to smolder as a foreign name is touted as a probable suspect in the terrorist attack. Preparations for war are made by the people in charge; the rest of the nation is preparing for a candlelight service.

Neighbors and strangers come together, people are kinder, more introspective, more patient.

Nobody talks about the weather.

A week later we are still in shock. The grief process is just begun. You don't have to know someone personally to be affected.

In my naive way I am stunned to read of a woman going door to door asking for donations for the Red Cross, then running away when asked for further information for giving blood. A local bar is broken into the day after the "bombings"; how far away I am in the understanding of those who can prey on others at such a time. I will pray for them.

Friends comment that all we can do is pray—I remind them of the power of prayer. Yes, we can and must pray. Hold the Light. This is what Spirit tells me in the first days of my grief for all who have died and for all who are left. "What can I do?" "Hold the Light. Just hold the Light. Do not wonder what it will do, how it will help, just focus all attention on holding that Light."

At the beach, with *Mama Cocha*[42] lapping at my feet, I feel the serenity and eternal movement of the waves. It's nice to know some things don't change. No matter the stupidity and arrogance of Man, the waves, for now, continue to lap at the shore.

42 Mama Cocha: the ocean.

Refuge for the Many Souls

Querido Waiki,

My friend Mark, in his Spirit form, assisted some of the souls who died on September 11. He led them to a place of respite, using me as a facilitator. What divine joy to assist at such a time of pain; it made me feel useful when I felt immobilized by confusion and grief. It was truly an honor to participate in this progression of souls.

September 19, 2001

Your birthday is today, my dear friend, Mark. September 19, a week and a day from our nation's enormous tragedy. In a way I'm glad you're there and not here. I know how deeply this would have affected you. At the same time I could use some really irreverent humor right now. Being in the form you are now, you can help even more than before. You can help us in a way I can't, and you can help those who were yanked so quickly from this life. Please help them.

I walked with you today to my special spot where you left me last in the form of a cougar. It seems long ago, in the snows of February. Hard to believe it has been only seven months. Not able to think of rebirth so soon, my thoughts were absorbed with death. A friend lies dying, convinced she will cure herself as soon as she works out her issues. Thousands died last week and my thoughts flit to a comment Liz made to me yesterday. "If you want to *do* something, connect and help those souls who were pulled so quickly and unexpectedly from this life. When you're doing your work, help them." I pondered how I could do this. What could I do?

Almost finished with my walk, I was stopped by an unusual noise and listened. My attention was drawn to a large, old cottonwood tree, with the upper limbs blowing in a peaceful breeze. "What, old tree?

What do you have to tell me?" There was an impression of refuge and multiple, peaceful souls. Easily I moved into meditation and asked for your assistance. I knew I needed your help to guide the souls of this enormous disaster here.

"We offer you this place of refuge, this place I cherish, with the green, gentle grasses, the rustling of the trees, this quiet, restful place. We offer you this sanctuary for as long as you need it." Spirit propelled me slowly in a circle, arms outstretched as I felt the entry of a vastness of Spirit. They had arrived, with Mark leading the way. "Thank you, Mark. Lead them here, keep them comfortable and safe until they are ready to move on." I continued moving in my circle. It was a slow, deliberate circle. It is movement that takes no effort on my part, nor any strength to hold up my arms. It is the circular dance of Spirit.

Contemplating my experience the following day as I talked to Mark, I asked, "Who else would die on the same day of the month as his birthday, but you?" Then, of course, the seventh month anniversary is on Mark's actual birthday. Surely there was a significance. The number seven is too significant not to be. Death, birth, rebirth, the number seven?

Not having a book on numerology, I thought of not only the next best thing, I thought of the better thing, or more appropriately, the better whom. I called Liz. "She'll know the answer to this puzzler," I thought. She chuckled quietly at my question and said, "Listen. This is how a musician would interpret it." I heard her fingers strike the keys of the piano. Recognizing the notes, I heard the rising cadence, "Do, re, mi, fa, so, la, ti . . . ti, ti, ti." No do. Her voice returned. "The number seven wants to go home, to rest. I love you." Click. Rest, Mark. You've earned it.

E-Mail to Survivors

Dearest Waiki,

A collective Spirit spoke to me recently, after the attacks on our country. This was a message sent out on the Internet to many friends via my e-mail, a message of Spirits' asking.

Dear All,

Some of you know me, some of you don't. Those that do, know the purity of my intent and Love for all things. If someone has sent this along, have faith as they do. Please read this message from Spirit that I was asked to move into the world. It felt as if the enormity and speed of the Internet was the best way to touch all involved, especially the grieving survivors. Putting the message into its proper context was necessary. If this reaches one person that it needs to, then I've done my job. If nothing else, enjoy the story. Many blessings and many thanks.

Marilyn Markham Petrich
Prescott, Arizona

September 25, 2001

The morning was sunny and warm, the heat of summer dissipating as the gentle warmth of fall made itself known. Walking briskly in this favored spot, doing my best to take in the beauty without halting every few feet to gawk, I was stopped nonetheless by a group of squirrels playing chase. Or was it a territorial dispute, I wondered? Silently I watched them, six in all, as they chattered and chased each other from tree to tree, branch to branch, racing in circles, up and down, all of them joining in. No, definitely not a problem with territory. I laughed aloud as I moved on, sorry to leave their antics, but needing the exercise just the same. A small pool crossing the road was beginning to recede due to lack of rain, a common occurrence in central Arizona. At least 50 butterflies of different varieties were disturbed as my walk skirted the water, the drone of bees and flies engulfing me for a brief moment as I passed. "Can't stop," I told myself, "I'm out for exercise today!" Difficult to do in this magical forest near my home, but I focused on another pool as my objective, one that is always full due to runoff from the lake, and quickly moved on.

Upon reaching my goal, I marveled again at such an exquisite place so close to my home, yet it feels so far away from the frenetic world. The water trickled gaily into the pool, the pine trees seemed to soar into the sky from their placement on the hill, while the granite rocks provided the perfect tumbling slide for the water to fall into the shallow, clear pond. The previous week had found me in this spot, engulfed with the Spirit of those who had lost their lives on September 11, 2001, a day none of us will forget. The trees spoke that day and I listened. The tall cottonwoods had sought to provide refuge for the souls of that tragic day, in this dear, sweet place, until they are ready to leave. A place of sanctuary. Joining with the trees in this offer of refuge, we felt the inrush of their souls and the contentment of their Spirit. Today I meditated here and felt the presence of Spirit and was grateful for the love of Nature and her thorough understanding of All in the Cosmos. Giving thanks in prayerful meditation, I turned to leave.

"Wait! Don't go yet!" I paused and returned to my place of quiet to hear what these souls had to say. "Let everyone know we are all right. Let all the survivors, especially our loved ones, know we are in a place of sanctuary and quiet. We will leave when it is time, but for now, we are here." My breath was sharp and full on the intake as I reeled at the importance of this request and I responded in my mind with, "But that is so BIG!" The concern of what others would think crossed my mind as quickly as a bolt of lightning, and the retort from this vastness was, "It is only BIG if you fear judgment." The truth of that statement sunk in as I began the walk home and was reassured I would have help, as always, with the reporting of these facts.

"Fear is the absence of Love" (Don Américo Yábar), the credo I live and love by, guides me as I move this message of reassurance into the world. I would ask that you, too, do not fear, have faith and reassure all you know who have been affected by this disaster. There are always larger forces at work and we must hold strong to the teachings of all the Masters, and the knowledge that Love does, indeed, conquer All.

MMP

To Go Beyond God

Dearest Waiki,

Many religions and cultures speak of God and Goddess. The predominant Judeo-Christian belief of my culture speaks of God as wanting to be praised, followed, adored or worshiped. The idea is, if we follow God's rules, as set down in the Bible, we will live in eternity with God in a blissful place called Heaven. I have a number of problems with these beliefs.

First of all, why would God, if God is all-knowing and omnipotent, need to be worshiped? That implies God has an ego. If God created all and knows all for all time (a man-made construct), I really don't think She'd have an ego about it. In addition, it is arrogant to think that with one life that averages 76 years, we can change everything at the last moment. In some fundamental belief systems, we can renounce all we ever did in our pitiful life at the moment of death, take Jesus as our personal savior and go live in Heaven with all the angels and saints! You can do this as a Catholic, too, except a priest must do it for you. The problem is, as a devout Catholic, you can light lots of candles, go to Mass every day and never skip communion. Then, one day, while helping an old lady across the street, you get hit by a bus and die. Well, because you never received Last Rites or confessed that piece of chocolate you ate during Lent, now you have to stay in a place called Purgatory until someone upstairs decides you've burned enough to continue toward Paradise. At least that's what I was taught. Obviously, the Protestant approach seems the better deal, but regardless of which religion you belong to, if you don't belong to theirs, you will burn in Hell forever! Daily, it becomes easier for me to toss aside my cultural restraints and be grateful for the sun and the moon, the earth and the stars that literally make my existence possible.

Contemplating the God question in meditation one afternoon, a different kind of revelation came to me. In my vision, I was looking out at the edge of the Universe, and the edge, with all its stars and planets, kept moving out and away from me, looking like an elliptical sphere. I came to know this edge as a symbol of God. As it moved away, I raced to catch up with it. As I raced, it raced too, then the edge slowed a bit. The next thing I knew, I was catapulted out beyond this edge into a great nothingness. The void was absent of color but had a definable space. The Great Nada, as I call it, had a very reassuring feeling.

It came to me then, why would God want us to come back to Her, to join with Her? Why would God (a term that holds strong vibrational energy) have us reiterate back to Her what She already knows? If God knows all, then God knows there is always more to know. What if God wants more from us? If we are all energy, if we all have life, then we are all children of Goddess. And what does that make God, but a parent? And what parent doesn't want more for their children? To learn more, to have more, to be more! To go beyond God, to learn more, so we can, in turn, teach more to God! In addition, if we all have souls which are eternal, always have been and always will be, and these are the attributes we give to God, then we must Be God! So why do we want to go anywhere? We are always with God, God is with us, and we can all be in Paradise at any given moment. It is just the realization and the knowing that makes it possible.

As you remind us, Waiki, there is nothing new under the sun and this was not my idea. It is an awareness, like many others in the Collective Consciousness, ripe for the picking, waiting for a picker of fruit. An apple, anyone?

Intent

My Waiki,

There was always great discussion when spending time with you about the difference between intent and intention. You explained it many times in different ways. I watched as some in the group would have the "Aha!" look on their faces while others continued to look confused. The intent of the work, as I understand it, is what makes it happen or not. It is absolutely essential not only to have intent, but to live with intent, and focus your intent. In the healing arts, you must have intent for the cleaning rituals, healing with stones, or any process of assistance. For me, I focus my intent to be of assistance, asking for the best outcome for the individual. Then, asking how I can be of service, Spirit guides me and tells me the intent to hold.

Preparing myself one evening for a talk I was giving on the Q'ero and the Quechua people, along with tips for listening to your heart and body, my mind turned over your example of intent versus intention. As you often do with groups, you related a story to more strongly emphasize a point.

You told us that as a youngster, you skipped school one day. On the streets of Cuzco, whom should you run into, of all people, but your father! You have described him as a very fierce man, certainly not someone to catch you playing hooky. He gave chase and you ran. You ran, unfortunately, into an alley with a six-foot wall at the end. With your father closing in, your intent propelled you over the wall, and you were safe. Later, you took your friends back to the spot and, try as you would, could not get over the wall. This is intent, you explained. Intention, the desire to scale the wall, would have you still at the bottom, not sailing over the top. That is the difference. Intention is the desire to do something, intent is the actual doing.

I searched my mind for a more current, cultural example I felt my audience could relate to. My solution was this: Intention is sitting in your car, idling, in neutral. Intent is foot on the gas, flying down the road! One is wanting, the other is already a done deal. Hope you like it.

Who Are We But the Laughter and the Tears?

My Dearest Waiki,

We are coming to a close on this aspect of our journey together. Mulling over all the different topics I've covered here, I again hear the excitement in your voice as you urge me to "Write about everything! The mountains, the children, the birds, your people, your life, everything!" I would say this poem has all of that.

Carla and Daniel held retreats in the forest near Carla's home. Carla has beautiful titles for her retreats; this one was called Voicing the Heart: Reflecting Your True Identity. *Together, they secured a scholarship for me so I could attend. I was touched and grateful. As a group we had a splendid but difficult time revealing who we are behind the masks we wear.*

At the end of the weekend, we went into the forest to meditate on our true identities. The prose below is what came to me and what I later ushered in with ceremony and the assistance of the group.

What is My True Identity?

We whisper on the wind, the words to hush the restless child.

I become the voice of Spirit I hear so clearly.

The soft, downy feathers of my wings tickle the boy playing with his dog, to hear him laugh just that much louder.

I am the salty tears coursing down my own face, remembering the Beloved's laughter.

We are the tree that I rest my back upon, feeling its gentle sway that provides my wind for the clouds.

The filth of mankind deposits itself into my grimy gutters.

I am the *Pachamama* who thirsts for the same debris, desirous to transform it with Love.

The Light that does not reach me, the angel wing that does not touch me, the serial killer who ends life as someone knows it—I am all and none of these.

How many feeble titles will you attempt to wrap around my Oneness, my Godness, my enigmatic condition?

The wind and clouds are mine as they are me; the woman who takes pleasure in the pain of others; the hard stone as it tumbles down the swollen river; all variations of Me, the Being, the Reality, the enormity of the atom, all Me. All You, all Us.

The possibilities endless, the questions fathomless, maybe I am simply a messenger to show you who You All Are.

And in doing so, Become Whole, Once Again.

A messenger simply brings messages. The message is maybe a smile, it may be Love, it may be Fury. As many beings, entities, thoughts and possibilities as there are in the multiverse, there are messages. And messengers. Mine is a message of Love, wrapped in Love, kindled of Love.

At times the message must change to suit the situation, so please don't kill the messenger. But if you do, remember the message, for it will never die.

Because energy is alive and has Life. Together in the Cosmos it will dance, in the endless ballet of the Eternal flame of God.

With Love as its partner.

Dedicated to Anita Louise West and Albert Handell, two fellow travelers who have touched my soul deeply. Through their art and their beings, others can see and feel Spirit as She moves through our lives.

Miguelito and the Coca

Waiki América,

On my recent trip to Salk'a Wasi, *amidst flickering candlelight and a small offering of Sambuca, four of us scrunched together at the end of the large dining table for Don Miguelito to read the coca leaves. You and Miguelito sat together at the end as Carla and I sat on each side, waiting patiently. Curious certainly, but patient just the same. This was my first experience of a personal divination with coca. I had witnessed the Q'ero throwing coca leaves the few times I had met with them. On the first encounter with these magical people, the leaves were thrown both to evaluate the auspiciousness of the meeting, and to determine if the* paq'o *Don Benito Machay was ready to be initiated into the next aspect of his training as a* pampa mesayoq.[43] *After the determination was made, we had the honor to witness a ceremony no white person had ever seen before. I'd observed other times, too, as you watched over the shoulder of another mystic throwing the leaves, while I watched the animated conversation and wished I understood* Quechua.

With simple ceremony, solemnity and laughter, Miguelito graciously assisted us as we ventured through this mysterious world with intent and curiosity. I watched as he threw various combinations of leaves; a clump, then three, then three again, then two, then one. There seemed to be a method, but one that followed energy and the moment, not a prescribed routine. Bent over the small pile of leaves, the two of you intermittently ruminated over the configurations, chuckled at times together, then outright laughed as you translated for me Miguelito's remark that I was married to a man "¡muy macho y bruto!" Well, that got some chuckles from the two of us also, as we had to concede that there was some truth to that divination.

Following your suggestion to Carla, I also asked three questions of the

---

43   pampa mesayoq: one who works with the energies of the earth and Pachamama, has an indirect relationship with the supernatural, but his or her main relationship is serving Pachamama. An expert healer, a curandero.

coca and Miguelito. *The three questions were to concern the* yachay,[44] *the* munay[45] *and the* llankay.[46] *Concerning the* llankay, *my first question was about a warm, powerful sensation I feel in my belly. I wanted to know how to elicit the feeling more, and how to use it, as I knew it was good for my physical body and my work. Again the leaves were thrown in combinations and discussed. Again you translated Miguelito's* Quechua *into* Spanish.

"First, you must immediately do an offering to the Pachamama. *It must be an offering to* Pachamama *for the land,* la tierra. *Then, you must meditate more with your womb and the moon (*Mama Qilla*), and do more meditations with your mind and the stars. You have received two answers in one! Now for your question of* munay."

"Waiki, there are many times my heart feels so big, so full of love, of sadness, of all the emotions of the world, I feel everything, and I know I need to open more. How can I do that?"

Miguelito grunted and smiled slightly as the leaves were thrown quickly and efficiently. With the tenderness of a Master, he spoke clipped and quickly. "Your heart knows many things." There was no need for discussion.

Later, by myself, under a full moon and rising mist, I gave an offering and many thanks to the Pachamama *for Her constant and reassuring existence. It was correct to give thanks for all She gives us: Her foods, Her beauty, Her many provisions and in the Andes, Her* Apus *and Her coca. I especially wanted to give thanks for someone like Miguelito, someone with such a strong connection through the plant, to remind me how to move while I live here within Her breath.*

---

44   yachay: knowledge, wisdom, intellectual power.
45   munay: heart; love, feeling.
46   llankay: ability to manifest in the world, the ability to express physical power.

The Mists of Salk'a Wasi

Stealthily and with quiet intent, I crept through the house. My purpose was not to be secretive; only to be alone. It was past midnight. Three others slept in the rustic old adobe house. Or did they? Américo often walked the night, especially when in the mountains of his ancestral home. I would have to be *salk'a* to avoid discovery.

Tiptoeing in my boots, I moved sideways where the floorboards creaked. The ancient blue door squeaked on its hinges as I tried to open it quietly. Glass panes in the upper section rattled loudly in my ears. The bottom of the door scraped against the damp wooden floor, and I froze, listening. I had not been detected. I stepped carefully onto the concrete step, mossy green and slick. It had rained every day of our visit, and the dampness was omnipresent. Following Miguelito's suggestion that evening, to give an offering to the *Pachamama* and meditate with the moon and the stars, this was my time to be alone, free from the energy of others.

Moving away from the house, toward the grove of massive eucalyptus trees, I came to the top of the worn stone steps, now slippery from the cool mist that hung in the air. I gasped at the sight before me. Nearest to me, the clumps of green grass and shrubs filled the small clearing, their shadows made comical by the full moon rising behind me. Beyond the grasses, there was a short, broken-down stone wall, illuminated with the brilliance of *Mama Qilla*.[47] Far below the wall were the fields of corn, *cevala* and potatoes glistening in the moonlight.

Like iridescent wool hanging in the valley between the towering mountains, obscuring the mountainside and river below, was what I can only describe as an apparition. A cloud of mist, moving with life, rose and fell, tendrils escaping the central core, and slowly crept up the valley toward me. Inexorably, methodically, with seeming purpose, it floated to where I stood. I remained motionless, caught in the mist's energy.

47   Mama Qilla: the moon.

Then, stepping carefully, out of respect for the night, I moved into the cloud, though I felt transfixed by the river of vapor, half expecting a boat or magic carpet to appear and carry me away. My boots and pants brushed the wet grass, and the moisture moved up my legs. Only my mind was attentive; my body felt swept away to a different reality. Secondary to all that I saw and felt, feeling myself grin with delight as I reached my destination, I sat on the crumbling wall.

Moisture caressed my face; the vapor moved in and around me. The dampness was like the lips of a newfound lover, the kisses freckle deep. Thinking suddenly of Conrad Aiken's *Silent Snow, Secret Snow*, I was alternately embraced and teased by the moisture. My head turned slowly and I watched the fog move up and envelope the trees; as I turned back I saw it just topping the house. Mesmerized, we—the apparition and I—fluctuated with the movements of the moon and the stars. Still my head twisted, slowly, smiling, taking it all in, watching the reversal of the breath that moved the cloud downward, until again it obscured the river below.

I performed my ceremony. My offering was accepted.

Spring Always Comes

My Dearest Waiki,

In the beginning of these stories, my personal life was a mess. Now I live with such a profound sense of joy and appreciation for all that there is, it oftentimes makes me weep. I have found true spiritual and romantic Love, and the delight of having them together.

I have resolved differences with friends and family, and still recognize the difficulty, along with the necessity, of doing so. And in recreating these relationships, I gain a deeper knowing of Love, and I hope, humility.

The lack of trust in myself and my own inner voice formed the haunted life I led. Now, the Divine voice is my guide. It is also my assistant and my source of inspiration, in times of creativity, as well as in times of despair and uncertainty.

Yes, even with bliss, there is sadness and pain. But the realization that, after all, tomorrow is another day, always stands at the forefront of my awareness, and for me, the exquisite gratification of being and loving far outweighs the temporary discomfort of the opposite emotions.

Waiki, you have helped me return to my own wisdom and connection with the power of Nature and the Cosmos. The power and humor of the Universe is constantly rained down upon me, as I sit in rapt wonder, amazement and gleeful adoration, at the myriad choices She offers us. She offers us the choice to be happy or to be miserable, to be in love or to be in hate, to give life, and to take it away. She offers all these choices with no attachment to outcome, and allows us the same possibility. We can choose to wander the forests of darkness, or return to our castles of wisdom. It is our choice, but one that impacts all the other beings of the Universe, much as the pebble in the pond.

If we choose to live a life of conscious connection to the Infinite, we must do so with Love and intent. When we live our lives moment to moment, with every one of those moments imbued with the intent of our purpose, we illuminate corners, caves, and whole worlds of darkness with the bright Light of wisdom and God.

Love and intent. The hallmarks of a life well lived. And think, we have so many miles to travel yet, so many souls to touch and be touched by, it is but a beginning. Another beginning. So many beginnings in the endless cycle of death and rebirth. I think I'll sit back and watch for a while. It's time to listen.

Epilogue

Below is additional information about Don Américo and ongoing work with the Q'ero and Mollamarka Indians of Perú.

"Don Américo Yábar is an internationally recognized Peruvian mystic and poet. Initiated by the Q'ero as a young man, he is a *chakaruna*, or living bridge of feeling between cultures. A master in moving energy, he is particularly adept in guiding Western minds in opening their hearts to connect their filaments with the Cosmos. Don Américo and the Q'ero have been written about in *Standing Stark* and *Calling Our Spirits Home* by Carla Woody, *Keepers of the Ancient Knowledge* by Joan Parisi Wilcox as well as articles in *Shaman's Drum* and many other publications."[48]

Currently, I manage a project of connection and Love, working with the Club of Mothers of Mollamarka, a small village of Quechua people in the highlands east of Cuzco, Perú. I am assisted in this work by DuAnne Redus and The LifeWorks Institute, a 501 (c) (3) organization, www.thelifeworksinstitute.org/home.html#indian.

The intent for this project began with the desire to ensure an adequate, clean source of water for the village of Mollamarka. The villagers are a shy, loving people who love others because we are humans on the same planet, and who live in union with the earth. They have lived this way for more than five hundred years, and we will continue to approach them with respect and honor for their way of life.

Due to my respect for their way of life, the project has evolved to supporting the Club of Mothers, an established organization in the village that helps the poor of the community. Working with both the Club of Mothers and the medical post, we encourage a holistic approach to health, both physical and spiritual, according to their

48   www.kenosis.net <http://www.kenosis.net>

traditions. We wish to assist the village only if they desire the change, recognizing change takes time. We also support the continued use of the local shamans and healers, and contribute toward the education of young people who choose to follow this path. This project is a gift of ayni, or reciprocity, for the unconditional love and service the people of Mollamarka have shown me. Beyond the work of the paña, the rational world, my intent is to be in connection with my spiritual people, and for the movement of Love and energy on the planet for the benefit of all.

In addition, I am working with Carla Woody of Kenosis as a translator and general assistant for trips to Perú to continue the work with Don Américo. "Carla Woody is the founder of Kenosis, an organization supporting human potential and spiritual emergence. Called an *angel of light* by the Andean people with whom she has worked, she is a teacher of conscious living, artist and author of the book *Calling Our Spirits Home* and *Standing Stark*. Carla has steeped herself in the world of Andean mysticism for nearly a decade and integrates it with her work in other spiritual traditions and NLP. She is highly skilled in translating the mystical for its transformative powers and grounding it into everyday reality."[49]

You may contact either of us at the addresses below.

Carla Woody	Marilyn Markham Petrich
Kenosis, LLC.	Inti Wasi Publications
P.O. Box 10441	408 South Alarcon Street
Prescott, AZ 86304	Prescott, AZ 86303
928-778-1058	928-445-9646
www.Kenosis.net	amaru@cableone.net
	www.intiwasi.org

---

49   Ibid., Kenosis.

Glossary

aini, ayni	Reciprocity. More than giving and receiving, in the Andes it refers to the constant reciprocal relationship with Pachamama and the Cosmos; always being in connection and gratitude. Socially, it is neighbor helping neighbor. And lastly, if one person knows more than the other, or can best another at a task or competition, one person shares their knowledge with the other, thus putting them on equal footing.
ánimu*	A subtle cosmic energy that exists in humans. When a child is born, it enters the top of the head and warms the child's blood, giving life. When we die, the ánimu leaves through the top of our head and blends with the cosmic weaving.
Apu*	The spirit of the mountain, a masculine energy, the receiver of celestial forces.
bruja	A witch. As explained by Don Américo, one who casts spells with bad intent.
coca q' awaq*	A master of reading coca leaves, a clairvoyant. Involves knowing how to use the coca leaves, how to see energy fields to read connections within the magical fields of action, and the appropriate use of energy.
despacho	Ceremonial offering.
filaments	Similar to, but not, an aura. All living things have filaments, and it is possible at times to see them. We can also feel and send filaments from a distance.
hamqui espíritu	A ceremony to increase another's ánimu, or life force.

hucha	Heavy energy. The opposite of sami, light energy. In the Andes, the Indians do not differentiate between good and bad energy, simply light or heavy energy. Heavy energy can make you feel unsettled, ill, or out of sorts. In our Western culture, we are touched every day by heavy energy. Thus, it is important to clean your energy body every day.
kuraq akulleq	(Also just 'kuraq') A great visionary who works primarily with the hanaq pacha, the superior atmosphere, with the celestial filaments, the heavenly energies. Very prophetic and charismatic; can heal at a great distance. There are only twelve of them in the Andes. The man is more visible to the outside world but it is usually the woman who moves the celestial filaments of energy. There are two levels of kuraq above this, but they cannot be named.
la gente	The people.
llankay*	Physical power; one of the three aspects of existence in the Andean cosmovision. The ability to manifest in the world and the ability to express.
lloq'e*	The left side, the mysterious, the enigmatic nonordinary world. It connects you to the mystery, the enigma, and with the unfolding of unknown energies which are present in all beings.
Lloq'enacuy	Cleaning ceremony done primarily by women. The intent is to clean hucha from the body and push the individual to the left, the lloq'e, using yarn to symbolize a feather, a feather that connects us to the Pachamama and the Cosmos. The hucha-filled yarn, when the ceremony is completed, is run to the closest source of natural running water, so it may be carried to the ocean to be cleaned by Mama Cocha.
Mama Cocha	The ocean.
Mama Qilla	The moon.
Mama Tuta	The night.
mesa	A Peruvian weaving, used often on the ground for ceremony. Also a place to store special stones used in healing work.

Mollamarka	The village above Don Américo's home.
munay*	One of the three aspects of existence in the Andean cosmovision. Represented by the heart, love and feeling.
NLP**	Neuro-linguistic programming. NLP studies how individuals learn, communicate, change and heal. With NLP, we can understand how people process, code and store information or experiences in their minds and, as a result, how these thoughts and beliefs manifest in their live communications, behaviors and bodies. Once these aspects are understood, an NLP practitioner has numerous tools to facilitate positive change and growth.
pacha kuti*	Kuti means to turn over, to change positions, the change for levels of consciousness. It means profound alterations, the emergence of the core structures of the universe. The pacha kuti is the time of coming transformation, a time of great upheaval and change; the end of history as we know it, the stepping outside of time.
Pachamama*	The spirit of the earth, the Cosmic Mother, the mother of all mothers. Mother Earth is female energy. She works with the blood, with birth, and she labors with death.
paña*	The right side, ordinary cultural reality. The logical, everyday, ordinary world.
paq'o	Spiritual leader, or healer, of the Q'ero, similar to, but not the same, as a shaman. A shaman works with plants and the energy of the plants. In the highlands of the Andes, there are no plants, just stones. So the paq'o works with stones, their energy, and the energy of the Cosmos.
pisco	The cane alcohol of Perú. Soda pop and pisco (or other alcohol) are often enjoyed when working with the Q'ero and participating in ceremony. Every opportunity to come together for the purpose of salk'a is always a celebration.
p'uncos	Pools of energy.
Q'ero*	The only remaining Incas in Perú. Five hundred

	years ago, at the time of the Conquest, these people fled to 17,000 feet in the Andes to keep their traditions intact. They have the least contaminated tradition left in the Americas. They are the keepers of the ancient prophesies. They believe they hold keys that will be important for the evolution of the world. They refer to themselves as "the people of the mountains and the stars."
Quechua	Indian language of the Andes. Spellings of words vary.
q'uyas*	Power rocks for use in healing and therapy. Learning to transmit energy, power and healing through stones is an important part of a paq'o's training. There are many different q'uyas with as many different applications. The q'uya is a rock that has a certain feeling; that has been charged with vital energy and with which you have a personal relationship.
salk'a	Wild, undomesticated energy. Our vital connection to the Cosmos.
Salk'a Wasi	The house of undomesticated energy. Américo's ancestral mountain home.
waiki	An affectionate term, meaning brother, or sister. It can be all encompassing, brothers and sisters of the world, united by salk'a.
yachay*	One of the three levels of existence, refers to knowledge, wisdom and intellectual power.

* Reprinted with permission, Oakley Gordon, Ph.D.
** Reprinted with permission, Carla Woody, MA, CHP